HIGHER STATUS

Higher
STATUS

The New Science of SUCCESS
and ACHIEVEMENT

JASON CAPITAL

HIGHER STATUS

The New Science of Success and Achievement

ISBN 978-1-61961-599-1 *Paperback*

978-1-61961-598-4 *Ebook*

CONTENTS

———

INTRODUCTION

———

I had heard about him for months. Some people said he was a genius, a playboy, or some combination of the two. But opinions are like nostrils, right? Everyone has at least two. I had to see with my own eyes what this guy was all about.

I watched him closely as he stepped on stage as a coach in front of hundreds of dedicated fans, guiding everyone from millionaires and A-list celebrities to authors, artists, and computer geeks. I saw a guy that seemed incredibly happy traveling across the world with his longtime girl-friend and closest friends. When it was time to return home from beautiful vacations to places like Bali, Thailand, and Rome, he boarded a jet to Newport Coast, California, back to his mansion overlooking the Pacific Ocean.

This guy had it pretty damn good. How did it happen for him? How did this twenty-seven-year-old kid with a high school diploma and no college degree accomplish so much in such a short period of time? After all, this was a guy who had been sharing a 500-square-foot apartment with roommates and unsuccessfully nagging the landlord to fix the broken air conditioner.

How did he transform himself from a painfully shy, unhappy, low-status person with floundering relationships, no money, and no future prospects to an inspired, high-status multimillionaire with great relationships, boundless energy, and a team of more than 200,000 people spread throughout 125 countries who trusted and followed his every move? He wasn't just living a high-status life, but he was reaping all of the benefits that came with it. I was completely fascinated.

It's surreal for me to sit here and try to understand the truth about this particular guy. Why? Because he's me. His story is my story, but it can also be yours.

HOW IT STARTED

At twenty years old, I had never had a girlfriend. I had barely even kissed a girl at that point. I was a six-foot-tall, healthy, good-looking guy, but I had big problems with girls. I was incredibly shy and just never knew what to say around them. My solution was usually just to avoid them at all costs. The possibility of rejection scared the shit out of me.

I had just transferred to Michigan State University, my fourth college in four years. A lot of my good buddies went to MSU, and they were pumped to take me to my first frat party. I had heard all of their stories about parties and girls, but it was finally my time to experience it.

We got to the frat house, a huge, 10,000-square foot building with three floors full of alcohol, drugs, and inebriated college kids. I was decked out in what I like to call the "average person uniform," which consisted of a nice button-up shirt, blue jeans, Vans shoes, and gelled-up hair. This outfit screams conformity—I was a sheep following the herd. My friends all looked the same, but I quickly learned they had far surpassed me in the social scene.

Within five minutes of arriving at the party, my friends had already started talking to a group of girls. Three minutes later, one of my buddies had one of the girls thrown over his shoulder, spinning her around as she giggled. Another friend was breathing fire out of his mouth as another girl applauded him. These guys just had it rolling—they knew exactly what to do. One by one, they each paired up and left the party until it was just me and the last girl from the group, a cute Midwesterner with blonde hair and a little button nose.

"Shit," I thought to myself. "I guess I've got to try to talk to her."

I approached her and ran through the same boring interview process that dooms most conversations with new people.

"Hey, what's your name? Where are you from? What's your major?"

It was terrible—just the most clichéd questions you can ask someone. Of course, I wasn't really interested in the answers, and she could tell. After about thirty seconds, I noticed her eyes darting around the room, looking for anyone else she could talk to.

"Listen, it was really nice meeting you, but I've got to go find my friends," she said as she turned her back.

In less than a minute, I had gone from meeting a girl to having her walk away from me, leaving me alone with only my red Solo Cup to cling to. At that moment, I knew I had to change something.

ATTRACTING ATTENTION

As soon as she walked away, I bailed on the frat party and sprinted directly back to my apartment. I was frustrated, I was embarrassed, and I was tired of failing. Something had to change. I set a new, bold personal goal: to become the world's greatest seducer. I know, I know, it sounds a little puerile, but that's how motivated I was to become more self-confident around others. I gathered all the psychology material I could get my hands on and immersed myself in learning about the ins and outs of both male and female psyches. Polarities, spiritualities, energies, sexual chakras—you name it, I read about it.

A few weeks later, I returned to the same frat house, only this time I was prepared with new techniques, tricks, and talking points. And guess what? It worked, because I was actually able to hold a conversation with a girl for a few minutes. It was progress. The following weekend, I was able to land the phone numbers of not one, but two girls in my apartment building. More progress. I was getting pretty damn good at talking to girls, but it still wasn't perfect. I had no trouble talking to most girls at parties or at bars—unless they were stunningly beautiful. If I felt like a girl was way out of my league, I had no chance.

Someone had to be attracting these girls, right? Once I started to pay attention to the kind of guys that dated these girls, it became clear: they didn't use any special techniques or pickup lines, and they damn sure didn't need to consult textbooks as thick as phone books for advice. So, what was different? It was simple, but I had never thought to look for it before: they carried themselves differently. They moved differently, looked at people differently, and spoke with a different tonality than the average person. There was a certain calm and cool demeanor they exuded, and girls picked up on those little subconscious signals. I also noticed the most successful, respected, and sought-after girls exhibited the same traits. It wasn't a coincidence. I didn't realize it at the time, but that was my first introduction to the idea of "high status." These people were literally broadcasting the high-status signal to everyone around, and it was responsible for all the great things they were going to get and achieve in life.

One of my favorite quotes comes from Jerry Sternin, who helped pioneer the concept of positive deviance. He said, "It's easier to act your way into a new way of thinking, than think your way into a new way of acting."

In other words, what you do is more important than what you think. That was the difference between me and the other more confident, more successful guys. So many of the self-help books and personal-development gurus available today focus on changing our beliefs and what to think, but, in reality, it's our actions that matter. It's not what we think or say, but what we do, that makes all the difference.

Look, like I tell all my clients, it's important to be honest. Most people say they don't make snap judgments about others, but the truth is everyone does. How do we make these snap judgments? By looking at the actions and behaviors that signal status. Does this make us bad people? Of course not.

Scientists at Harvard and Oxford have only recently discovered this is a natural part of our brain's protective functioning. It instinctively tunes into the status signal another person is sending out, and it quickly decides whether that person is high status or low status. Winner or loser? Someone I'd like to do business with or not? Someone I'd like to date or not? Someone I would hire or not? It's in understanding or resisting this one fact of life that getting your dream life either becomes very easy or very hard.

Understand: the psychology side of success and achievement—that's a small side dish. The juicy steak, the main course that's going to feed your spirit and help get you the life of your dreams on a silver platter, is your actions, your behaviors, your status signal.

With this new knowledge fueling me, I decided to try a little experiment. First, I dropped all the pickup techniques I had taught myself over the previous few months. The guys I had been watching didn't need them, so why should I? I then asked myself two questions: What celebrity or public figure do I personally, truly admire? What celebrity or public figure does the opposite sex seem to be attracted to? Take a minute to think about your own answers to these questions. It doesn't matter if you're male or female, having a high-status person to study and model yourself after is important.

At the time, *Iron Man* was a huge hit and it seemed like every girl I knew thought Robert Downey Jr. was the hottest guy they'd ever seen. I admit, *Iron Man* is my favorite movie of all time, but I defy anyone to find a film character comparable to Tony Stark. You've never seen anyone carry himself the way he does in that movie. He's one of a kind. The way he moves, even things as subtle as a slight turn of his head when his assistant-turned-love-interest Pepper Potts comes downstairs to his workshop stood out to me. He doesn't drop all his work the second Pepper enters the room, because he sees himself and what he's doing as extremely valuable. That's a high-status mind-set. Someone with a low-status view of themselves would drop what they're doing immediately. If Tony Stark is in the middle of something, he will take an extra ten, twenty, or thirty seconds to finish before slowly turning his head. It's calm, it's controlled, and it's at the rate that *he* wants to move.

What that does is frame the interactions between Tony and Pepper. He's essentially saying, "I'm not more important than you in this situation, but I am establishing that I am important and what I'm doing here matters. You're going to have to wait a second." That's entirely physiological. He didn't use affirmations or incantations or change his entire way of thinking. He simply changed the way he acted, and suddenly, she responded to him differently, with more respect for his time and attention. One little change in his status signal and her entire view of him changed.

The next time I went out, instead of trying different techniques or specific lines, I just carried myself differently. I modeled Tony Stark, a guy that succeeds with the type of women I wanted to attract. Your model doesn't have to be a film character played by Robert Downey Jr. As a woman, it can be someone like Beyoncé. Who it is doesn't matter, as long as you have someone to model. From the moment I accepted that, everything changed. It was like night and day.

I had a paradigm shift in my understanding, and it was incredible. It felt like I had unlocked a secret truth that most people couldn't understand. I was in uncharted territory, like I had the answers to a test others didn't even know existed. Of course, people eventually started to take notice, and that had both positive and negative consequences. I started to draw more attention from people, which was great—except for the hate from some of the Michigan State fraternities. A lot of the girls at their parties became more interested in me than any of the frat brothers and, well, they didn't exactly appreciate that.

I wasn't always an enemy though. One of the frats had a forward-thinking brother in its midst. Instead of just talking shit about me from afar, he approached me and basically recruited me.

"We've seen you around," he said. "We know what you do. Here's what we want to do. We'd like you to come to our frat a couple hours before our big party, we'll gather all of the brothers in the living room, and you can bring a whiteboard and show us some of your secrets. We want to learn."

The same guy who was getting rejected and ignored by people only a few months prior was now being asked to teach an entire fraternity. You can't make this stuff up.

"Of course," I said. "That sounds fantastic. Let's do that."

I worked with a number of different frats, sharing everything from my views on status and charisma to conversation techniques. They ate it up. They loved it so much, in fact, that they started telling their friends outside the frat about me. Eventually I had guys coming to my dumpy little apartment on Friday evenings and paying me $20 to drink with them while I showed them stuff on a whiteboard.

As word of mouth began to spread, I started getting clients outside of just college-aged kids. Men in their thirties, forties, fifties, even sixties. Doctors, IT guys, entrepreneurs, and other successful people who just struggled with confidence and talking to women.

The more time I spent with my clients, the more I realized I had not only a special talent for teaching, but for helping guys achieve great results. I absolutely loved helping people: it was a high I'd never felt before. For instance, I had a client tell me recently that since he began working with me, the revenue of his company increased by 400 percent. And, by the way, his company was already bringing in $18 million annually before he met me. Stories like that fuel me, and it makes me excited for what is possible for you.

What quickly became the most interesting aspect of my clients' results was the wide-ranging scope of influence. The guys I worked with found they were getting the results they wanted with women and in their social lives, but they also noticed they were getting different results at home and work. Fathers began to notice their children listening more attentively to them. Employees began to notice they received better reception and treatment at work. Female executives started to notice more respect from their employees, without having to feel like they were overcompensating.

It had become crystal clear: all of the status I was teaching wasn't just for getting girls. It became a highway to getting whatever you want, whether it's someone from the opposite sex, money, fame, freedom, prestige, ascension—literally anything you want to do. Status became a unique tool, separate from the sea of books, seminars, and experts focusing on psychology. If studying those materials is like filling your car with gas, then working on your status is like upgrading the engine. You tell me: wouldn't you rather be driving a new Ferrari instead of taking the bus with everyone else? We're focusing on what actually matters, and that's what makes all the difference.

THE POWER OF STATUS SIGNALS

Being high status has absolutely nothing to do with money, cars, clothes, titles, or shiny things. That's the biggest misconception about high status. Those material items are just ornamentations that give off false status signals. Material possessions are the opposite of honest signals, which evolutionary psychologists define as something that can be easily spotted and can't be faked.

Honest signals indicate our status level, and high status opens the door to many benefits in life. Some of those benefits include:

- **Effortless attraction from the opposite sex:** You never have to worry about whether someone is interested in you or not. According to Dr. David Buss, author of *The Evolution of Desire*, "Women in the U.S. do not hesitate to express a preference for mates who have high status." That door swings both ways: men also prefer high-status women.
- **Increased financial stability:** High-status individuals are the highest-paid people on the planet, regardless of their field. A study conducted by researchers at Duke University's Fuqua School of Business found that CEOs with a higher-status vocal tonality made an extra $187,000 on average

per year. You'll never have to worry about your bank account running low again.

- **Increased attention at work:** Quicker promotions and bigger salary raises are more common for high-status individuals.
- **Better relationships with family and friends:** Parents are able to develop more meaningful relationships with their teenage sons and daughters. You command respect and become a leader in your social circle.
- **Increased networking opportunities:** Connecting with people at events, galas, industry parties, and other conventions becomes easy. The best networkers and most connected people on the planet are all high status.
- **Planned purpose in life:** You gain a fulfilling sense of purpose and excitement about where you're going. Total freedom and control over the direction of your life becomes a reality. Life becomes fun again. What could be better than that?
- **Unexpected perks:** You'll start to get personal upgrades at restaurants, clubs, and airports for seemingly no reason at all. This happens to my clients and me all the time.
- **Health benefits:** High status has been shown to correlate with human longevity and health. Research has shown that animals with lower status die sooner,

contract more diseases, and recover more slowly than animals with higher status. Humans are no different. You will live longer, be healthier, and have more energy.

- **Increased loyalty from loved ones:** Whether you're a man or woman, you'll be able to inspire unwavering loyalty and devotion from your significant other. The harsh truth is people rarely leave high-status people: they leave low-status people.

Don't be hypnotized by the mainstream media into thinking that higher status means possessing scarce resources like a Lamborghini, Rolex watch, or a $5,000 Chanel bag. That is complete bullshit. Status must be learned, not purchased. Dr. Buss says, point blank, "Status and possession of resources are separate qualities." I can't state it any clearer myself.

Many of my clients ask me if they are too old to become high status. They fear that old dogs can't learn new tricks. Again, that's bullshit. Neuroscience has discovered that the human brain is highly plastic, meaning it can be re-formed and new behaviors can be learned at any age. Status is all about behaviors. We're not going to think our way into a new way of acting: we're going to act our way into a new way of living. It doesn't matter if you've spent all sixty years of your life being low status. Give me a few days to flip you to high status, and you'll immediately begin to gain control over your emotions, relationships, and destiny. Don't you want to be living the life of your dreams? Of course, you do. Let me help you achieve it.

The American public bore witness to a powerful example of status signals during the infamous 1960 presidential debate between Richard Nixon and John F. Kennedy. Nixon appeared sweaty and weak, and lacked good energy. We know now, of course, that he was battling the flu, but millions of television viewers had no idea. They just saw someone who looked low status, especially compared to Kennedy, who was younger, stronger, and more confident: he epitomized high status. Despite Nixon's lead in most of the preelection polls, it was Kennedy who became the thirty-fifth President of the United States, and his televised display of high status played a major role in that outcome.

WHO IS JASON CAPITAL?

I get a lot of labels thrown at me—teacher, guru, marketer, speaker. Others just call me a world-class salesman with nothing to offer. I've heard them all. If I *had* to define myself with a single title, it would be "coach," but I always remind my clients of a simple yet effective saying: labels are fables. Don't allow yourself to be boxed in by other people's definitions. You need to determine who you are and who you're going to be in this world every day.

I have served as a coach and consultant to everyone from Fortune 500 executives and professional athletes to *New York Times* best-selling authors and award-winning Hollywood executives. I was recognized as a top 100 entrepreneur by President Barack Obama, and I've received more than 10,000 success stories from clients around the world. I was put on this planet to make people high status, and help them obtain all of the incredible things they want and deserve in life. And that most certainly includes you.

Everyone needs a mission in life, a greater purpose. We all need something that pulls us forward. A lot of people ask me, "What is your mission with Team Capital? What are you doing with this book? What is the ultimate goal?" My mission is to transform one hundred million people into the highest-status versions of themselves.

When I transform one hundred million people into higher-status individuals, there will be a massive downstream effect that affects everyone in their path, almost like an invisible hand. Instead of existing as a boring cog in life's spinning wheel, the high-status version of yourself will stand out as an inspiring, charming, charismatic, loving, and caring human being who is amped up about life. And on top of all the incredible benefits you'll reap, it's also going to have a positive effect on your family, friends, and coworkers. It could illuminate their own path to high status.

This book is for anyone who has any desire to be more than they currently are. Most people are happy with the way they are. They're comfortable, and they give in to the pull of the familiar. Most people are content to simply wake up, eat a boring breakfast, get in their boring car, drive to their boring job, do boring work for eight hours, have boring conversations with their bored coworkers, drive the same boring route home, where they may or may not make boring, routine love with their significant other before falling asleep in a boring bed. Wash. Rinse. Repeat.

People are bored. People feel stuck. And many have already given up on themselves, while others are just waiting for a miracle that's never coming. Consider some of these horrifying statistics:

- Americans spent $70 billion in 2016 on lottery tickets. They spent $55 billion less on books.
- Nearly 50 percent of all marriages worldwide end in divorce.
- According to a study, the average American watches

more than five hours of TV. Per day. Even worse, according to another study, when given the choice of watching TV or spending time with their father, 54 percent of kids chose TV.

Emerson once famously said, "Most men lead lives of quiet desperation." He wasn't wrong, but it isn't just men who are losing their extraordinarily valuable lives right before their very eyes. Men, women, and even children today are increasingly leading lives of quiet desperation, and the crisis is only picking up speed. You see it all around you: people's lives slipping from their grasp, yet they don't have the power to stop it. We now live in a world where not being high status will hurt you, frustrate you, and have you spending years going nowhere. That's why the successful breakthrough science shared inside this book has already transformed the lives of thousands worldwide, with hundreds more joining every day. And you, my friend, are next. So, turn the page. Let's get to it.

Chapter One

BECOMING HIGH STATUS

When I was thirteen years old, I made a pact with my closest friends to play on the eighth-grade basketball team. We all played together on the weekends and, at least skillwise, were about on the same level. We all went to tryouts together. Everyone had a great time. I couldn't wait to play on the same team with them—it just felt right.

The coach posted the roster list in the locker room the next day. I couldn't control my excitement. I sprinted past my friends, who had already seen their names on the list. They were high-fiving each other, talking about what numbers they were going to wear on their jerseys. As I scanned the list, I began to feel sick. When I reached the bottom and didn't see my name anywhere, it crushed me. I was convinced it was some sort of mistake.

I rushed into the coach's office and asked what happened. All I got from him was, "Sorry, Jason. Better luck next year." That was it. I felt overwhelmed, so I sprinted straight home. I burst into my bedroom, teary-eyed and heart-broken. To my thirteen-year-old self, it was the end of the world. All of my friends made the team and I wasn't going to be able to hang out with them every day. I was going to be alone.

What happened next is difficult to explain, but it felt like a spark of lightning from Zeus in the clouds. The tears stopped and it hit me like a ton of bricks. "Fuck this," I thought. "I'm going to play college basketball." It was a ridiculous dream, of course. I wasn't even five feet tall, weighed less than 100 pounds, and had maybe a six-inch vertical jump. I did not have the factory-installed parts that are normally found in college basketball players.

One thing I had that few others did was an ability to become obsessed with a subject—in this case, basketball. Over the next five years, I spent every free moment I had in the gym, making a thousand shots each day, going through ball-handling drills, and scrimmaging. Nothing could stop me from playing college basketball. By my senior year of high school, I was one of the top point guards on the travel basketball circuit and I ended up getting recruited to play at Eckerd College, a Division II school in Tampa Bay, Florida.

When I got there, it was fun at first, but I felt so burnt out. For years, I had spent thousands and thousands of hours pursuing this dream of playing college basketball, and when I finally achieved it, it felt empty. I realized I was never going to be this all-time great player. I would never have the natural ability to play in the NBA, but I knew I had the ability to develop a healthy obsession with—and eventually master—a singular subject. That's what I did with basketball.

THE NEXT STEP

I might not have had a shiny new NBA contract after hanging up my basketball shoes, but I had major confidence that I could learn and master any new skill. When I moved back home and transferred to Michigan State to reunite with my friends, I was ready to immerse myself in something new. After my experience at the frat party, I began poring through books on everything from psychology types and cognitive biases to seduction books written by Italian author Giacomo Casanova. As I mentioned earlier, I was intrigued by Jerry Sternin's belief that it's easier to act your way into a new way of thinking than to think your way into a new way of acting. Millions of people try to improve their lives daily by changing their thinking, when the truth is they'd get there much faster if they focused on improving their actions. With better actions comes better thinking. The more insights I absorbed, the more I began to formulate my own ideas.

Posture, body language, eye contact, tonality, charisma, storytelling, even breathing—these are all small things that people don't focus on, but greatly affect the impression they make. I'm going to share a quick but incredibly important science lesson with you now: pay close attention and take it to heart, because it will be a theme we revisit throughout this book. When someone meets you for the first time, their subconscious will immediately decide a few things about you. It doesn't matter if it's your coworker, a first date, your grandmother, or a complete stranger. The first decision is whether you are safe or a threat, and this happens in less than one hundredth of a second. If you're out with a group of friends and a big, scary guy walks in wielding a machete, it doesn't take you a couple of minutes to analyze the situation. You know immediately that your safety is being threatened.

The second thing people will decide about you, after determining you aren't a threat to them, is what your status level is and how it compares to theirs. They will instantly assess whether your status is higher than theirs, lower than theirs, or about the same. This is a survival mechanism that has been ingrained in our subconscious for hundreds of thousands of years.

How does someone know if another person is high status, neutral status, or low status? We can make a determination thanks to the twelve honest signals of higher status. Evolutionary psychologists have researched animals, from peacocks to gorillas, and concluded that they display honest signals. These signals allow animals to display their status level to potential mates or others in their tribe or territory. For instance, a male peacock will spread its wings to attract a mate. Female peahens will choose their mate based on the color, size, and quality of the feathers. That is an honest signal: a peacock can't fake its feathers.

Human beings attempt to cheat this with Lamborghinis, Louis Vuitton heels, and other lavish material items. They are trying to signal high status with those types of trappings, but those are not honest signals. We don't trust those. Our subconscious hasn't been trained to accept a $5,000 Chanel bag as an honest signal. This is why you can see a high-status person, like Elon Musk or Robert Downey Jr., with a $100,000 Tesla or Lamborghini and think, "Yeah, that makes sense." But if you see a video online of someone you don't know with a Lamborghini, it will feel like something is off. That's because Musk and Downey are truly high status on a subconscious level, while the other guy isn't. How can our brain tell? In a fraction of a second, it gauges for a mix of the following twelve signals:

1. Destiny
2. Body language
3. Voice
4. Eye contact
5. Walk
6. State control
7. Carefreeness
8. Truth
9. Rapport control
10. Charisma
11. Style
12. Environment

Once you have mastered all these honest signals, everyone you meet will instantly recognize you as high status. You'll become naturally unforgettable, develop magnetic charisma in both your personal and professional lives, and enjoy deeper, more meaningful connections with your partner, friends, and family.

STATUS HIERARCHY

Every single person carries with them a map at all times. Not a physical map, but a status hierarchy that includes every other person they meet. We're constantly making these instantaneous readings of people, every time we enter a new environment or context, deciding if they're high status, medium status or low status, and they are doing the same with us. Everyone wants to know where they stand in the status hierarchy, from the boardroom to the bar to family picnics. We are constantly making these judgments in our life. This is an evolutionary mechanism, but how do people decide where to place you in their hierarchy? What affects this split-second decision?

Keep in mind that the human brain is not a camera. It does not take perfect pictures of the external world and file them away for future viewings. The mind cannot capture exact images: instead, it labels. Again, the labels we're looking for here are high status, neutral status or low status.

I've had many people disagree with me about the human brain. They'll say, "People aren't that shallow. They shouldn't judge. I don't judge." I don't laugh in their face, but honestly, that's just nonsense. Snap judgments happen all the time, even unintentionally. Is this a cool person? Is this not a cool person? Is she a punk girl? Is he an athlete? We are constantly looking to label people. This quick, snap-judgment labeling is known as invisible status judgment. Ninety-nine percent of people never learn to understand this, but the lucky few who do have been thriving with it for centuries.

These instant snap judgments allow us to turn on the TV

and, when we see George Clooney, recognize him immediately as high status. A guy like Artie Lange, for instance, we know is low status. It's the same difference between a high-status woman like Oprah Winfrey, and someone like Lena Dunham, who is undeniably low status. You just know it when you see it. It's the same snap judgment that lets someone know whether you're attractive or not, lets the boss know if you're worthy of a promotion or not, and makes an audience love you or forget you.

People might only look at one or two of the twelve honest signals of higher status to make this snap judgment. This is normal. It's also not uncommon for people to have a few signals that are more polished than the others. In that case, we want to broadcast those as clearly as possible to ensure you're constantly being perceived as a high-status individual. Every snap judgment will come down to these honest signals, and those will determine everything that happens to you in your life.

THE GREATEST TRUTH OF ALL TIME

Remember this next sentence—circle it, highlight it, write it down, save it in your phone. The world will accept the judgment you place on yourself. It's worth repeating: the world will accept the judgment you place on yourself. That, my friends, is the greatest truth of all time.

Whatever message you convey with your tonality, eye contact, body language, style, charisma, state, mood, and energy, among other signals, will be received by everyone you meet. They are gathering a judgment of yourself from you. If you see yourself as an unworthy, low-status, low self-esteem person, that will permeate all of your sub-communications and prevent you from living a life that energizes you, that you truly love. If you place a low-status judgment on yourself, you will continue to drift through life without a true purpose to fuel you.

On the flip side, if you see yourself and carry yourself as a high-status, high-value, high-self-esteem individual, that will shine through in everything you do. Without verbally stating anything, you are communicating to the world that you are high status, and others will treat you as such. You'll be viewed as a leader instead of a follower, someone who commands respect from your friends, family, and coworkers. You'll evolve from someone that exists in the background of rooms to the most memorable, desirable person in every room you enter.

THE PATH TO HIGH STATUS

Before we go any further, I want you to take a moment and make a decision. Becoming high status is a choice, and it's one that only you can make. I can't make it for you. Mom and Dad can't make it for you. Your kid, your significant other, your friends—none of them can make it for you. You *must* make it for yourself. I'm going to show you how to do it, but the first step is making the decision.

This decision will require what's known as a self-image switch. How you judge yourself, your own self-conception, the idea of yourself—this is your self-image. This is basic psychology. Dr. Maxwell Maltz wrote a great book titled *Psycho-Cybernetics* that takes a deep look at self-image psychology. In it, he wrote, "Self-image sets the boundaries of individual accomplishment."

This is a simple, yet profound concept. If you see yourself as a person who can only make $10,000 a month, you will never make more money than that. Your own self-image determines the limits of your accomplishments.

Another powerful example of self-image comes from Keith Johnstone, one of the greatest innovators of improv. In his book, *Impro: Improvisation and the Theatre*, Johnstone tells the story of the improv class he taught in the 1960s. He tried over and over to get the actors to portray strong, powerful characters, but they could never get it right. Eventually, he tried a different angle. "Just try to get your status level a little bit above your partner's," Johnstone told them. That was his only cue, and it changed

FAST ACTION EXERCISE: STATUS VAMPIRES

As you continue to increase your status every day, you're going to realize that it takes energy. It takes energy to accomplish anything important in life. The things that rob us of energy are what I call "status vampires." If you don't have your status vampires under control, you won't be able to do anything effectively.

We have many, many, many of these status vampires that continually drain our energy. Maybe you started a workout program or signed up for a kickboxing class, but you only attended the first session of a four-week program. A week later, you might find yourself thinking about it. Status vampires are secretly there in all of us, slowly sucking our energy all day long. When you start something in life but don't finish it, it sticks with you, inhabiting your subconscious.

It's like running your computer with fifteen programs open in the background. How's your computer going to operate efficiently with that much of an energy drain? Human beings are no different. So, how do we combat status vampires?

STEP 1
For the next six minutes, I want you to write down *everything* on your mind. Leave nothing to waste: get it all out of your head and down on paper in front of you.

STEP 2
Now, mark an X beside each item that robs you of the most energy. These are your status vampires. There's something called the Pareto principle, which typically finds that, in most things in life, about 20 percent of the activities can account for 80 percent of the results. It will be no different with your own list. Twenty percent of the items you just wrote down are robbing you of 80 percent of your energy. Identify them and put an X beside them.

STEP 3
Now, write down an actionable step you can take to put closure on each of your status vampires. Status vampires are, by definition, things we have started but haven't finished. If you signed up for a workout program but have fallen behind, commit to catching up and finishing it. Or instead, start a new program you know you can finish. Either way, you are closing that status vampire. It will no longer consume energy by taking up space in your mind.

An alternative to closing a status vampire by completing it is to simply let it go. Consciously say to yourself, "This isn't helping me. I just have to drop it." If you've been thinking about the workout program, but it's just not something that's important to you, let it go. Get it out of your mind. By reducing—and eventually eliminating—status vampires, you will see a massive return of energy.

everything. Intuitively, all of the actors understood what it meant to be higher status, just like they understood what it meant to be lower status.

Johnstone's improv experiment reinforces this simple truth: you already have all of the tools you need to become high status. What you must do is honestly identify the status level you have been assigning yourself. What level have you maintained, but more importantly, what level will you reach now? That is the key question.

The only thing I need from you right now is your final commitment, before we take the first big step in the next chapter. Do you want to become a person of influence, someone who lives a passionate, driven, and exciting life? Do you want to wake up every morning ready to *attack* the day with every ounce of your being? Do you want to stop spinning your wheels and start spreading your wings? If so, that journey starts right now. You must commit to becoming a high-status person for the rest of your life, not only for yourself and all the achievements you will garner from that decision, but for your kids, friends, and family as well. They will be inspired by this massive change in you, and you will feel that response.

With that is going to come a lot of responsibility. Imagine it: you're going to become a beacon in your social circles, a leader in your family, and the center of your community. Sure, that's a bigger weight to carry, but it's also an enormous source of power for you. You're going to become the rare, standout superstar that can effortlessly inspire change, make a real difference, and leave a lasting impact on those lucky enough to be involved in your high-status journey.

You might not know where that journey is going to lead yet, and that's OK. Actually, it's better than OK—it's awesome. Picture it: as everyone else continues to go nowhere and do nothing while following the same old clichéd advice, you're entering a new world where you're about to discover the true success technology that only a privileged few have ever encountered. Your life is about to take off like theirs did. Are you ready? It starts right now with your high-status destiny.

Chapter Two

HIGH-STATUS DESTINY

When we think about high-status individuals through-out history, there is a common thread among them all. Whether it's a great king from antiquity, the leader of a conquering army, like Alexander the Great, or a CEO of a major corporation in modern times, they all display high-status destiny. These people were *born* to be a king, queen, conqueror, or CEO.

They have a grand, unique purpose for being on this planet. They know why they're here and what they're meant to do, and therefore don't deal with the uncertainty others do. So many people spend their entire lives feeling like they have no purpose, no great reason why they were born. That's especially true nowadays in a world populated with 7 billion people. A lot of people find their sense of belonging through family and friends, others through their work, but that can often be a shallow distraction. At the end of the day, when they shut off the TV and close Snapchat, Instagram, and Facebook, there's an empty feeling. They feel alone. A lot of people purposely avoid reflecting on this because it's scary as hell to think your life has no deeper meaning. The population is the highest it's ever been, which makes it easy for people to feel a sense of insignificance, like they don't really matter. But that couldn't be further from the truth.

Times are different now than they were thousands of years ago. You and me and everyone else on the planet, we don't have the benefit of being born with thrones to inherit or kingdoms to rule, and we probably don't have family money to rely on. We're just regular people, right? But that doesn't mean we can't find, create, or claim our own purpose for being here.

When you do discover your high-status destiny, you'll recognize a change in your daily life immediately. You'll feel excited, passionate, and truly alive, like you've been filled with an energy you never even knew you had. Instead of waking up in the morning and thinking, "Oh great, another shitty day to get through," you'll say, "Hell yeah! Let's go, this is awesome." You'll also start to notice that other people will look at you differently. Everyone from the barista at Starbucks to your own family members will recognize the energy you emanate. You'll burn with a rare fire that everyone will immediately pick up on.

Maybe you already had that fire earlier in your life as a kid, but a teacher or a parent or someone else in an authority role extinguished it. Maybe they told you your dream, whatever it might be, wasn't possible, that it was just wishful thinking. When I look around the world today, everyone's fire is out. It's sad, but it doesn't have to be that way. Remember, your destiny isn't something you find under a rock. It's something to be created, nurtured, developed. You—only you—can grant yourself permission needed to start creating it now.

SHALLOW SUCCESS VERSUS DEEP PURPOSE

Many of you reading this book have already found success in your lives, and that's awesome. Maybe you're pulling in a nice salary, or have the nicest house on the block, or you just have a great social life—however you measure success, that's great. But what is your *destiny*? Success is easier to achieve than truly finding your purpose in life. My life is a perfect example of this.

When I was in my early twenties, I was making somewhere between $15,000 and $20,000 a month with one of the first online businesses I launched. I had a cool apartment in the Gaslamp Quarter of San Diego, and I was constantly meeting girls and making new friends. I thought I had it made. Literally, I felt like I was ready to retire. If I could have made that much money every month for the rest of my life, I was beyond content to live out my days hanging on the beach. On the surface, it all looked perfect, but in reality, something was missing: I had no purpose.

After a few months, the appeal wore off and, like anyone without a high-status destiny, I grew more and more miserable. Without a true passion, I drifted along until I picked up a new activity—smoking marijuana. I had never really tried pot up until that point, but one of my friends convinced me. The next six months were a haze, both literally and figuratively. I wasn't accomplishing anything, but being perpetually in a in a pot-induced, feel-good mood, I didn't give a shit. The highs offered a temporary escape, but when I reached the end of those six months, I was just a stoner with no money left in his bank account.

I mostly ignored the business that had been making me almost $20,000 a month, so of course it fell apart. I had no job, no money, and, worst of all, no passion. I had no destiny. I had to swallow my pride, pack up all my shit, temporarily move back home to my parents' house in Michigan, and just hope that I'd figure out the next step. I knew I had to give up the pot—that was an easy decision—but I was about to learn that I hadn't even hit rock bottom yet.

One of my first nights back home, some of my buddies from college hit me up to come out for some drinks. To them, I was the one kid in the group that had actually started to become successful and moved away from Michigan—to sunny California, no less. They had no clue the financial trouble I was in, and of course I didn't want them to know. I had to keep up the front.

When the time came to order the second round of shots at the bar, I stepped up. "Shots are on me!" I pulled out my card and handed it to the bartender like the rock star I was pretending to be. About twenty seconds later, he came back with the bad news.

"Sorry man, this card was declined. Wanna try another?" Shit. Not good.

I gave him a different card, but I already knew it would get declined. My heart was racing, my mouth was dry. I was just beyond embarrassed. "It's probably just the bank protecting me since I'm traveling and not in California right now," I told them, hoping they bought it.

Most of them didn't think twice, but one of my buddies saw through my act. He paid for the shots and pulled me aside. "Hey man, so you're living back home right now and your card just got declined. Is everything OK? You can tell me, it's cool."

In retrospect, that was such a great way for him to ask me. He genuinely cared, and he wasn't trying to embarrass me, but at the time, I couldn't accept that. I straight up lied to his face. "Business has never been better. I just wanted to spend a few weeks here at home."

The next morning there was a knock on the front door. I was the only one in my parents' house, so I answered it. There, standing in front of me in the doorway, was the happiest little girl I had ever seen. She proceeded to give me a well-rehearsed sales pitch asking for school library donations. The local elementary school needed new books for the library, so students were going door-to-door asking for, at minimum, $10 donations.

Being unemployed and broke, I had no money to offer this sweet little girl, but I couldn't tell her that. So, I lied again. "Hey, no thanks. I appreciate it, but I don't really believe in that sort of stuff." It was a stone-cold lie for the ages because I am absolutely obsessed with reading and learning: seriously, every room in my room is stacked with books. Her shoulders slumped and her eyes welled with tears as she turned and started walking to the next house. My heart sank.

I've never felt lower than that moment. I felt like complete shit. I was tired of being unemployed, tired of the numbers in my bank account looking more like than area code than a phone number, tired of lying to people—just tired of all of it. I decided that day that something had to change. Being unable to donate $10 to a local school was my "enough is enough" moment.

Finding your high-status destiny isn't necessarily going to involve visiting a crystal-ball reader, backpacking through Europe, or hanging out in the jungles of New Zealand until an idea comes to you. The first, and most important, step is simply deciding that enough is enough.

COMMITMENT TO YOURSELF

Are you excited by life? Do you feel alive and inspired every day by your pursuits? Or do you feel purposeless? Do you feel like you're just floating through life, like a leaf being tossed aimlessly by a wind you can't control? This is something only you can answer, and you have to be honest with yourself.

Maybe you've already decided enough is enough. Maybe that's why you picked up this book in the first place. If so, awesome. If not, don't stress. Everyone's "enough is enough" moment is going to be different. Sometimes it comes from listening to someone else, or hearing another person's story. My moment came when I had to lie to a little girl's face. For Michael Jordan—yes, that Michael Jordan—it came when he was cut from his high school team as a sophomore.

Long before he had six NBA championship rings and was widely regarded as the best player ever to touch a basketball, Jordan was just an undersized kid hoping to play for his high school's varsity team. When he didn't make the team, it crushed him, but he didn't wallow in sadness. Instead, it ignited a fire deep inside Jordan that propelled him to unmatched levels of greatness. The following year, he made the varsity team. Two years after that, he accepted a scholarship to the University of North Carolina. Three years after that, he was drafted by the Chicago Bulls and, well, the rest is history. But it all started with that "enough is enough" moment back in high school. You can have that moment *right now*. If you're tired of the same old shit and want something better, I'll help you find what you're truly destined for.

The truth is, when someone doesn't know what their

greater purpose in life is, they will lack aliveness. You can just tell by looking them in the eyes—they're not completely dead inside, but they're on their way, and it's kind of scary. I see it when I go to the grocery store, where obese human beings toss box after box of Twinkies and Twizzlers into their overflowing shopping cart. I see it when I go to corporate offices, where the receptionists are too distracted by their cell phones to greet guests. And I see it in far too many studies, like the one that found more children prefer TV over interacting with their parents. David Deida, an author who has written a number of books on the relationships between men and women, describes this perfectly. Deida writes, "Every man knows that his highest purpose in life cannot be reduced to any particular relationship. If a man prioritizes his relationships over his highest purpose, he weakens himself, disserves the universe, and cheats his woman of an authentic man who can offer her full, undivided presence."

Deida writes that from the perspective of a man, but the same is true for women: nothing should trump your purpose. The most important thing in life isn't what other people are doing on Friday night, how many likes your last online post got, or what's happening on *Game of Thrones*. It's your purpose, your destiny. If you ignore your purpose and continue to float through life, you're doing yourself an incredible disservice. But if you follow your purpose, you're making a true commitment to yourself. It's a powerful feeling. Trust me, I know from experience.

FOLLOW WALT DISNEY'S LEAD

A lot of people think that Walt Disney became immortal once he created Mickey Mouse, but in reality, his empire was still growing. He wanted to build Disneyland at a time in the 1950s when amusement parks weren't commonplace. He wanted to bring his passion to life and share it with everyone: that was his high-status destiny.

Others didn't see it that way. They told him he was crazy, that something like that would never work. He was turned down for financing over 100 times. When someone with no destiny in life is told they can't do something, they'll believe they can't and give up on it. Walt Disney was different. He had already tasted success with the creation of Mickey Mouse and Minnie Mouse and the rest of his classic animated characters, but he believed he was destined for more. When investors and other people told him they appreciated what he had done with the animation, but that they didn't think he could build a massive amusement park that would draw visitors from across the globe, he didn't take it as a slight. He simply thanked them and moved on to the next option. Destiny does *not* slow down.

When Walt Disney was younger, no matter where he was or what he doing, he was always drawing. Even when he was a teenager and in his early twenties, before he moved out to California, his coworkers noticed that he'd always be drawing at his desk. While they would spend their breaks playing poker or just hanging out, Walt would stay put and draw. What a perfect illustration of high-status versus low-status destiny. Maybe drawing started out as just a hobby for Walt, but it quickly became his passion and then a healthy obsession. It consumed him in a brilliant, positive way.

If you look at the most successful men and women throughout history, you will find this pattern among all of them. Everything they're doing and thinking, every conversation they're having, is based on their destiny. It all revolves around the big thing in life they're excited about. In today's society, you hear constant talk about a work-life balance. Bullshit. That was created by people who aren't immensely successful. It's an idea created for lazy people who lack ambition. In their eyes, the Walt Disneys, Steve Jobses, and Elon Musks of the world have no work-life balance. The truth is, they don't need a work-life balance: they love what they are doing so much that to put it aside would be a downgrade. It would make them unhappy.

Understanding your high-status destiny gives you a

laserlike focus in life. Dean Martin was notoriously laser focused. When he would get a new movie, he would tear out every single page of the script that had dialogue that didn't include him. Any time a scene that didn't involve him speaking was being filmed, he didn't know what the hell was going on. You can argue it's a bit narcissistic, sure, but you can't argue about his focus. Dean Martin was so locked in on his own lines that nothing else mattered.

WHY CAN'T YOU?

Walt Disney and Dean Martin and all of these other legendary people are great examples to look back on, but what about you? What's holding you back from realizing your high-status destiny?

It's *never* too late to change. Always, always remember that. Research has shown that neuroplasticity is a very real thing. Human beings' brains are highly plastic: we can learn new things, change our behavior, and ingrain new patterns of behavior throughout our entire lives. Your past doesn't define your future. Previous failure—or success—doesn't guarantee anything moving forward. Once you come to your "enough is enough" realization, you have to take an action toward changing your situation. That's when everything can start to change. Your past has nothing to do with that, unless you use the past as motivation.

Let's be honest: lives that are easy are uninteresting. Oprah Winfrey had an incredibly painful and traumatic childhood. She could have let those experiences define her life and set her on a much less glamorous path than the one she ended up on, but she didn't. She has a quote where she said, "I don't think of myself as a poor, deprived ghetto girl who made good. I think of myself as somebody who, from an early age, knew I was responsible for myself and I had to make good." She went through living in poverty, being sexually molested, and losing a child at fourteen years old, but she came out of it thinking, "I have to make good as an adult." That's pretty amazing.

Andrew Carnegie, who is one of the most financially successful men in the history of the world, once said, "The richest heritage a young man can have is to be born into poverty." It's one of my all-time favorite quotes. Here's one of the richest men ever, and he's saying the richest heritage someone can have is to simply not be born into a rich family. Someone who is born rich can't relate to not having money. They don't understand the fear of being broke.

I didn't grow up in a wealthy family, so I know what that's like. I know how it feels to have no money, and that keeps me going sometimes. I will never allow myself to go back there.

Sometimes I think about the time I had to move back home to Michigan. I remember being so broke I couldn't afford a cleaning lady to come to my San Diego apartment before I moved. I spent hours cleaning the place, including the marijuana ash stains in the kitchen. It was humbling, embarrassing, and, most of all, painful, but I never allowed myself to get angry. Even at the time, when, on the surface, I was at my lowest point, I knew it was going to make a great story when I eventually became successful.

I give this advice to a lot of people at my seminars, but I want you to remember this: one day does not make a lifetime. When you go through those tough moments, you will move past them. It's just one page in the entire book that is your life, and no one wants to read a book that's nothing but happy moments. Our own unique trials and tribulations are what make our journeys unique. Embrace them. Use them as a catalyst, so you can say, "Enough is enough. I'm never fucking doing that shit again, ever."

IMPACT ON OTHERS

One of my good friends recently had his first child. He's approaching his midthirties and I've known him for about a decade. I never thought he would have a kid, but now that he does I have to admit, he's a great father. He told me that the moment his daughter was born, a lot of the lesser priorities in his life just fell by the wayside.

Becoming a parent forced him to grow as a person, and he could no longer waste time on B and C priorities. His focus shifted to the A priorities, which are his family and his work. That's it—that's his destiny. Once that shift happened, the effects became pretty amazing. When he wasn't spending time with his daughter, he was working. Pretty soon, he began to make more money than he ever had. None of the other people in his local group of friends have kids, so they all just drift through weeks in search of the weekends, so they can get fucked up and forget how much they really don't enjoy their lives.

My buddy used to live like that too, but once he became a father, that changed. He gave up the weekend partying. He just doesn't have the time for it anymore. But once his friends saw how hard he was working, how focused he had become, how disciplined his life was, some of them followed his lead. His actions caused them to reflect and think, "Wait. I don't necessarily have to lead this boring, uneventful, uninteresting life like everybody else. I don't have to work a boring nine-to-five during the week and just go get drunk every weekend." It's a liberating—and infectious—feeling.

His friends decided to dedicate their lives to their passions, rather than remain in the week-to-week rut. They didn't look at my friend, the new father and hard worker, as selfish or narcissistic, but rather as a leader, a bright beacon to follow. He became a light that illuminated their path. What that does, of course, is continue the cycle: friends of theirs begin to see their change and follow them, and friends of those friends do the same thing, and so on. It's like a never-ending cycle.

High-status destiny also makes life simpler. How so? Research has shown that multitasking is not a desirable quality. In fact, it's a sign of low intelligence and creates stress. In the 1990s, multitasking was the shit. People would proudly announce on their résumés that they were "an excellent multitasker." That's great and all, except now we know the brain isn't designed to multitask. It causes stress, and that's not a good thing. When you know what your destiny is, life becomes a lot simpler. Rather than stressing over decision after decision, some far less important than others, you can just ask yourself, "Does this serve my purpose or not?" What could be simpler than one question? If the answer is yes, great. If the answer is no, don't waste your time on it. Simple. Clear. High status.

This decisiveness is simple, yet one of the most profoundly desirable traits on the planet. Humans typically like to follow people who are decisive. It gives us a sense of safety and comfort. One of my mentors, legendary businessman and coach Dan Peña, always says, "I may be wrong, but I'm never in doubt." Fucking classic. It's so true though: people will follow someone who's decisive, whether or not they're always right. Writer Elbert Hubbard once said, "Leaders are people who make quick decisions and are sometimes right." There's no hesitancy when you know what your purpose is. You might not always be right, but, like Peña says, you'll never be in doubt. That's such a powerful notion.

SET YOUR GOALS TOO HIGH

When Ted Turner's father died, he left behind two things for his son. The first was a $2 million trust fund, which is pretty cool. The second was just a piece of advice. He told Ted, "Set goals that you cannot achieve in this lifetime."

Let's be honest: how many people do you know that actually think like that? Probably no one. It's rare, and typically only found in those with a high-status destiny. When you have something big that you're working toward, something so big that you don't think it can be achieved in this lifetime, that turns you on. That's damn exciting. A great example of this is businessman and entrepreneur Elon Musk, who wants to put people on Mars. He's not even fifty years old yet, and that's a goal he may not be able to achieve in his lifetime, yet he's still working tirelessly at it.

P. T. Barnum is best known for cofounding the Barnum & Bailey Circus, but here's a quick history lesson for you. He was also the second self-made millionaire in American history, behind Ben Franklin. Pretty cool, right?

Barnum might be most famous for his circus, but he was a man of many talents and accomplishments. Case in point: his museum in New York City had 850,000 different displays. You read that right—850,000 displays in a single museum. Just think about that for a minute. It blows my mind. It's almost impossible to even imagine that many items in a single building.

The circus came later in his life, but there's plenty to study from his earlier years. Barnum is basically the father of modern publicity. The guy was brilliant. For him to gather that many items for display in a single museum, how central do you think his purpose was? How rampant was it in his life and his thought processes? That was all he was committed to in that moment, and it made him radically successful.

DON'T WAIT

How often do you hear people say, "I just need an opportunity?" All the time, right? Well, guess what? It's bullshit. While they're sitting around waiting for an opportunity to just come along, they're not preparing like they have a title fight coming up. So, if they're just waiting and not preparing, they won't be ready when they do eventually get a chance. Always stay prepared.

Robert Downey Jr. is one of my favorite people on the planet, and if you didn't know that already, you will by the end of this book. His life has been far from a smooth ride, so it's a good thing he didn't sit around and wait for his chance to break back into Hollywood.

It's well documented that Downey struggled with a drug addiction. He spent time in jail, got fired from *Ally McBeal*, and even bottomed out by mistakenly stumbling into a neighbor's house and passing out in one of their beds. His life was a mess for quite a while. Want to guess how much he made for his last *Avengers* movie? Only $50 million. That would have never happened if it hadn't landed the starring role in the first *Iron Man* movie, and that definitely wouldn't have happened if he just "waited for his opportunity."

Downey knew he was made for the role—it was his singular

purpose at that time—so he begged director Jon Favreau for an audition. Typically, established actors like Downey don't need to audition, but he had spent weeks preparing for it. From morning until night, he did nothing but rehearse and practice for the role. He said, "I felt like a fighter that was training for a title bout that hadn't been booked yet." When he showed up for the audition, his brain shut off and his preparation took over. By the time he was done reading, there wasn't a single person in the room who wasn't certain they had just seen Iron Man.

I know what you're thinking: Jason, that's an awesome story and all, but how the fuck can I compare to world-class actor Robert Downey Jr.? Easy—just think of the onion. No, don't start crying. The onion is unique because it has layers. Finding your high-status destiny is just like peeling the layers of an onion.

As you start down your own high-status path, you've got to begin with the low-hanging fruit, which is the very first thing in front of you. Even if you don't think it's your destiny long-term, attack it with 100 percent commitment. Don't put it off. By taking action now, you're moving forward. That's how you start. Eventually you'll begin to notice that you've become a stronger, smarter, better-developed person, because you're living life like a high-status individual. By attacking that one thing, you'll shed that first layer, and when that happens, you're in a new place.

For the second layer, attack the next thing on your path. Attack, attack, attack. Another layer will come off, and you'll evolve with each layer you shed. Each time you do this, you get closer and closer to the core of your onion, your destiny in life. I had to peel off multiple layers before I found my true cause. First, I thought I was going to play professional basketball, then I built my first online business, then I helped guys become successful and confident with women. Now I've reached my core and my purpose is something that would make Ted Turner's father smile: I'm going to make 100 million people become high status. Is that a goal I can achieve in my lifetime? Maybe, maybe not, but it consumes everything I'm doing and drives me forward. In fact, once your life changes for the better after applying the science and knowledge gained from this book, I'm going to ask you to help me with that. But not until I truly help you out first. Sound good? Cool.

RAFTING IN BALI

I went to Bali with my girlfriend for about two weeks in 2015. It's an amazing country, full of beautiful scenery and some of the happiest people you'll ever meet. One day, we went whitewater rafting. It was fucking intense. We're talking like four-plus hours of heavy duty, intensive rafting.

When we finally got to the end, everyone in our group was relieved. They were exhausted and wanted nothing more than to sit down and smoke a cigarette. Oddly enough, it seemed like everyone else in our group smoked cigarettes. They were *pissed* when they learned that our excursion hadn't quite ended yet. We still needed to carry our paddles and the raft up a massive, half-mile staircase back to the starting point.

Groans and profanities just erupted from these people, they were so angry. Me? I picked up my paddle and raft and started sprinting up the stairs. I have a high-status destiny. I'm excited about life, and I was excited about the new experience I was having in Bali. Why would I let some stairs ruin that? Everyone else was yelling shit at me as I sprinted past them, but guess what? That's going to happen sometimes. Just take that as a sign that you're doing things correctly—that you're on your high-status destiny path.

DESTINY IS A MUSCLE

People aren't born with certain abilities. No one is born to be a successful businessperson, an all-time great basketball player, or an award-winning musician. They have to train to accomplish these feats. The same goes for the body. No one is born with giant biceps, toned legs, or a great ass. You have to train those muscles. Your high-status destiny is no different.

It doesn't matter what layer of the onion you're in, you can attack it with all the strength you have, knowing that it's going to be building a muscle that will grow stronger. Each day you will become stronger and more powerful. A perfect example of this is Richard Branson. How many businesses has he built? Hundreds—everything from Virgin America and Virgin Records. He's constantly peeling off new layers of his onion with his continued dedication to taking action. Every time he starts a new business, even if it ends up failing, it wasn't a failure in his eyes. The point for Richard Branson was never to be a perfect businessman, but to have fun, make some money and help people.

FUNERAL EXERCISE

This is one of the major exercises I put everyone in my seminars through, because it helps point you in the direction of your high-status destiny. Imagine the following scenario: you walk through a dark hallway into a room you've never seen before, but as you enter, a bright light illuminates the entire room. As you take a few steps inside, you notice that a lot of the people you've known in your lifetime are there, and they're all dressed nicely.

You are invisible to them—they can't see or hear you, but you can hear and see them. As you listen, you notice they're sharing stories about times you were happy and excited. As you get closer to the front of the room, you realize you're in a funeral room—and it's your funeral. You do another few laps around the room and listen to more stories. People aren't overcome with grief that you're gone, but they're remembering all the good times. They're talking about you in a really positive way.

OK, now grab a pen and paper. It's time to answer four questions:

- What were they saying about you?
- What were the big accomplishments that you achieved in your lifetime?
- On a scale of 1 to 10, how do those accomplishments make you feel?
- If you were to increase any of those scores to a 10, what would have to happen? What would need to be different to raise the score?

By answering these questions, you'll have a list of accomplishments that you subconsciously want in your life. When we do this exercise, we're able to shed all of the expectations and rules that other people place on us. You can think clearly about yourself and your life. Now, you have a starting point, an unpeeled onion. This is the place to start building your high-status destiny.

But your destiny, as important as it is, is one piece of a larger pie. Your destiny will certainly fuel you and keep you energized on a daily basis, but how you broadcast yourself to others through your body language is another important aspect of high status. Can you become the highest-status version of yourself with weak, low-status body language? Have you been broadcasting low-status body language, without even realizing it, and costing yourself major opportunity after major opportunity? It's very possible, so let me tell you all about that now, starting with a fascinating body language discovery.

Chapter Three

HIGH-STATUS BODY LANGUAGE

Here's a fun stat for you: approximately 60 to 65 percent of all interpersonal communication is comprised of nonverbal behaviors or body language. Nonverbal communication can reveal a person's true thoughts, feelings, and intentions. In poker, we call it a "tell," right?

Isn't it interesting—I'd also argue alarming—then, that most people spend the majority of their time focusing on what to say, what to wear, or how their hair looks. Only 7 percent of interpersonal communication consists of actual spoken words, yet everyone focuses on what to say and what not to say. Seven percent for spoken words compared to sixty-plus percent for body language. It's not even close: our body language says everything about us. People understand instinctively that they can't always trust people's words or facial expressions, but we trust body language. We learn from an early age how to tell white lies and convey those lies with our faces, but we don't think about our bodies. Body language is an honest signal of status, and it's incredibly important.

Remember this next sentence—it's one of the most important things you can understand about your own body language. High-status people will make themselves comfortable first. This is a shocking distinction because we're taught to not infringe on anyone else's space—personal space, right? I'm telling you to take up *more* space. Human beings are most comfortable when they're expanded, when they're open. When you're a high-status person, the energy and attention in the room is typically centered on you to begin with. If you enter a room and immediately make yourself comfortable, it subconsciously gives everyone else permission to be comfortable as well. People follow the lead of high-status individuals.

UNIVERSAL LANGUAGE

People in China speak a different language than people in Switzerland, at least verbally. Physically, they speak the same language. Body language is universal and instantly recognizable. It's the language spoken all over the world, so it makes sense to become well versed in speaking that language. It's also easy to master. The problem is that no one is teaching it.

Seriously, there are so many self-help seminars being taught by life coaches that focus on changing your belief system. What a crock of shit. I don't know where that all began, but I really hope this book puts an end to it. Achievement doesn't come from the psychology of changing your beliefs: it comes from physiology. Always remember that. You need to have the physiology of a high-status person to ensure you become successful and become someone other people want to be around. We don't need to focus on journaling or affirmations or walking over hot coals to make that happen. All we need to do is move our leg a few inches to the left, put your arm over the chair next to you, and take a deep breath to relax. Boom. In ten seconds, your body language went from low status to high status. Change can be affected instantly with something as powerful as high-status body language.

If you need further proof, let me share with you a quick story about one of my clients. He's a sixty-six-year-old doctor with a PhD from Harvard who constantly travels the world with his girlfriend. He's been a number of my courses, so he came to understand the power of high-status body language. He saw it firsthand at a disco in Thailand.

He was at the bar with a few of his buddies, just enjoying a night out. There was a group of girls to their left that were being hit on obnoxiously and aggressively by another group of guys nearby. Understandably, the girls got sick of it, so they began talking to my client and his friends. The other group of bros didn't appreciate that.

"What the fuck do you think you're doing?" one of them said to my client's face.

My client didn't flinch. He didn't get nervous and fidgety, He remembered OGSP—which you're about to learn—and calmly replied, "I'm having a good time."

That was it. Five words. The other guy didn't know what to do. After a few seconds of staring my client down, he walked away. Even though this guy was thirty years younger and almost certainly could've beaten my client in a fight, he picked up on the high-status body language my client was displaying.

MORE BENEFITS

Social psychologist Amy Cuddy gave an incredible TED

Talk presentation on research into what she refers to as power poses. According to her research, if you stand in a power pose for only two minutes, you'll get a rapid increase in testosterone and a simultaneous decrease in cortisol. What exactly is a power pose, you ask? It's OPGS—being open and grounded, taking up space.

Our body language affects our hormones and the chemicals in our blood stream, which in turn affects our mind-set. When you enact this high-status way of living through just your body language, you become a different person.

It's pretty amazing stuff. You'll become more relaxed, feel more powerful, become more naturally assertive and gain physical benefits, just from enacting high-status body language in everything you do. You should always be aware of your body language, whether you're sitting or standing.

There are four components of high-status body language. Not forty, not 400—just four simple things to keep in mind. I want you always remember the acronym OGSP. Again, it's OGSP. The letters stand for *open*, *grounded*, *slow*, and *priding*. Let's break each one down.

OPEN VERSUS CLOSED

You can probably picture this in your mind already. The top sign to look for here is the distance between right and left joints. If your right and left wrists are close together, you're closed in that area. Same with your right and left elbows. Same with your knees, shoulders, and ankles. If your hands are crossed, that's another sign. If your arms are crossed, that doesn't necessarily mean you're closed. It's all about the context of your entire body and the space you're occupying. When you're closed off, you're signaling that you feel low status in comparison to others in the same room. This type of body language is opportunity avoidant and responsible for countless missed opportunities in people's lives.

On the flip side, a high-status person will keep their body open. Their right and left elbows, wrists, knees, and ankles will be farther apart. If you're sitting down, you might have your legs open a bit, or have your arm around the chair beside you. You're taking up more space without being obnoxious. You're indicating that you're used to the attention being on you, and for good reason: you're high status, and that's where the attention goes. That confidence shows through your body language.

GROUNDED VERSUS FLOATING

A high-status person will remain confidently grounded, while a lower-status person will nervously float around the room or fidget in their seat. Being grounded means your energy is feeding back into your body instead of your mind. It's being present in the moment, instead of time traveling to the past or the future. It means when you encounter a challenge or a trigger, you remain firmly rooted within yourself. You're strong, you're present, you're here. Now.

SLOW AND CONTROLLED MOVEMENTS, OR NOT

No one wants to be around someone who's fidgety or nervous all the time. It makes us uncomfortable. That's a low-status characteristic, and it's a huge turnoff. On the other hand, if you imagine someone with grace and controlled movements, they're signaling high status. Why? Because it indicates they are comfortable in that situation. Nothing fazes them.

It doesn't matter if you're in the boardroom or the bar: this is universal. Low-status people let nervousness take over their bodies to the point where they become almost unbearable to be around. We like to be around people who appear comfortable. A high-status person, even if they are feeling nervous, will still present themselves in a slow and controlled manner.

Imagine you're underwater. How would you move underwater? It's not super fast or fidgety, but more of a controlled, comfortable pace.

PRIDING VERSUS HIDING

Priding means exactly what it sounds like: you're damn proud of who you are and what you're doing. Someone on their path of high-status destiny is going to be proud of that, and it will be reflected in their body language. Imagine you just won the Super Bowl, or the NBA Finals. You wouldn't be playing small or hiding away, right? You'd be up, open, priding. You'd be comfortable drawing attention to yourself. You'd be so excited about life, you wouldn't even be thinking about it. High-status people are proud, and they've got nothing to hide.

Someone that's hiding is, again, doing exactly what it sounds like. They're wearing ill-fitting clothes and their body language is closed up instead of open. They're taking up as little space as possible. We pick up on all of these signals immediately. Closed, hiding body language is unappealing, but open, priding body language helps make you irresistibly appealing to the opposite sex.

I can write pages and pages about every single aspect of body language, but the most effective way to teach you to distinguish high status from low status is through visual aids. We had some fun here at the Capital compound and put together a quick little photo shoot to illustrate some of the key aspects of body language.

Take up more space: We already covered open versus closed, and this is basically the same idea. If you're closed up, you're taking up less space. By opening up your body, you'll be taking up more space. Take a look at the two accompanying photos. What stands out to you?

The body language on the right is high status, while the body language on the left is low status. In the right photo, the woman is clearly open, grounded, and priding, right? Compare that to the left photo, where she is closed up, not grounded, and hiding. She is not taking up her personal space.

Keep your head still: Fidgeting and other nervous behaviors are low status, and we'll explore more on those in a bit. Regarding your head, it's fairly straightforward: keep it still.

Keep the room in front of you: You don't need to be onstage to have the same effect as this photo of me at one of my events.

Any room where you can position yourself to have the wall behind you and the room in front of you will have the same high-status effect.

Wide animation: There's a difference here between a high-status wide animation and a low-status, over-the-top display. Keep your arms inside your own personal space, like I am doing in the next photo.

Note how I'm using my hands in an animated way, but keeping them within my personal space. Picture someone making a crazed, emotional, histrionic display and what their arms look like during it. They're flying all over the place, right? You don't want to do that. Moving your arms outside of your personal space in that manner crosses the threshold from wide animation of presentation to low status.

No fidgeting: Tapping your feet, cracking your knuckles, rubbing or wringing your hands together, touching your neck—any form of fidgeting you can think of is negative.

You've got to focus on eliminating it. Look at these next two photos. What stands out to you about them?

Which one of these photos is displaying high-status body language? It's the one on the left. That's a high-status hand position, in which she used her thumbs to gain an edge. In the other photo, she is wringing her hands in a classic low-status behavior.

Focus on the hands: You can say a lot about your status with just your hands. Get in the habit of practicing "steepling," which is touching all of your fingers at the fingertips to create a gesture that resembles a church steeple. The accompanying photos can be used as a reference.

Nonreactive to environment: A high-status person doesn't let their environment affect their body language. Whether it's loud or quiet, crowded or empty, hot or cold, it doesn't matter. You alone control your status. Later in this book, we'll take a deeper dive into high-status state control, which is the ability to control your state regardless of external factors.

Point foot away: Your feet are often one of the most honest signals of how you are feeling. When engaged in a conversation with someone, by simply pointing one of your feet away from them you will convey you have somewhere else to be.

It's not being rude. You just have to keep moving because you're on your path to your high-status destiny. This is something we will revisit in more detail in the chapter on carefreeness.

Sitting: Did I miss my calling as a model or what? I'll leave that up to you to decide, but in the meantime, let's focus on the high-status seated position on display in the next photo.

Notice how I'm leaning back and taking up my personal space by extending my left arm over the top of the seat next to me and placing my right arm behind my head. When we are in a fearful, low-status state, we tend to unconsciously cover and guard our torso area. Why? Because all of our most important internal organs reside there.

When we're feeling more relaxed and in control, we naturally lean back and open up our torso. It signals high status to everyone in the immediate area.

MAKE IT NATURAL

All it takes for you to learn a new standing or seated high-status position is one positive response. One source of positive feedback is all it takes for your brain to remember that position for future situations.

Let's say you're out at a bar and, since you've just read this chapter, you're being mindful of OGSP. If you strike up a conversation with a cute girl, you're not going to lean in closer to talk to her. Ladies, you know what I'm talking about. That's closed body language, right? Instead, you're going to remember OGSP and lean out. There's a very simple saying I teach all my clients: when in doubt, lean out. Remember that.

The next time you find yourself in a similar situation, your brain will recall the time you leaned out instead of leaned in. And what happens when you lean out? She'll lean forward because she's more invested in the conversation. That's a good thing. You'll start to get different responses than you've ever gotten before, solely because of your body language. A simple technique like leaning back can be insanely effective. Case in point: one of my friends utilizes the lean-out as his sole move during business negotiations, and he has more cash than he knows what to do with.

To make anything completely natural, you have to constantly practice it. You have to become a long-term student of body language to master it. Observe it, study it, notice it. What I recommend to everyone is to find two high-status models. One should be someone you don't know—an actor, YouTube star, TV star, something along those lines. The second should be someone you can see in person—someone in your office, at your gym, or at the local bar.

Watch the way they move, sit, and stand. Study them. If you're watching them on TV, try muting the sound and just focus on their body language. Pick up on their movements and practice them in your own life.

BODY LANGUAGE EXERCISE

I want you to go back through the high-status body language positions from above and choose just one. Pick the one you think is the most intriguing or, if you're really adventurous, the one the feels most unlike you. After you've picked one, I want you to focus on that position for one day.

On day 1, wherever you go and whoever you're with, just focus on mastering that one position. At some point in the day, it's going to feel right, and you're eventually going to get a positive response. It might be from a coworker, family member, or friend. It doesn't matter. What does matter is that your brain will file it away.

On day 2, choose another position and do the same exercise. Continue this until you've mastered all of them. In a little over two weeks, you'll have all these positions down, and it will completely transform the way people look at you and respond to you. Respect, recognition, attention, and more.

WHAT-IFS

There are a few scenarios I get asked about specifically by clients at my seminars, so they're worth highlighting here.

PEOPLE NOTICE THE CHANGES

One of the worst places to adopt new body language positions is with your close friends. You might not think that, since you're comfortable with your friends, but they will notice you moving differently.

"What is wrong with you?" "Why are you sitting like that?" "Why are you standing like that?"

Don't let questions like this make you uncomfortable. If someone says something like that to you, just reply back,

"Yup, I feel fantastic! Thanks for noticing," and then move on your way. Simple.

I'M AFRAID

This is normal. All human beings have fixed patterns of movement. Changing these patterns with new positions isn't always easy. It feels uncomfortable at first because you're so used to sitting and standing in a certain way.

What's important to remember in this case is that everyone around you, regardless of what they say, wants you to be high status. No one close to you wants you to be unsuccessful or less happy. Knowing that, you almost owe it to all these people who are close to you to increase your status as much as you can.

When you become higher status, you're going to be able to bring them into a bigger, better, brighter life. They're going to love it, and they're going to love you for helping them.

DON'T IGNORE YOUR BODY LANGUAGE

Your high-status future requires dedication to body language. You're not going to get there with low-status body language. It's just not possible. It's critically important that you make a commitment to increasing your high-status body language. It's an honest status signal that's there for a reason.

You weren't born to be low status, and the good news is that with even just one fixed position of movement, you can begin to reach high status. Now is the time to create better, happier, and more effective body movements.

At this point, you're attacking your destiny and you know how to improve your body language. How does it feel? Pretty damn good, right? Don't slow down now. The next high-status trait is one of the most genuine honest signals, so it's crucial that you dominate it. Let's do it.

Chapter Four

HIGH-STATUS VOICE

———

Margaret Thatcher, the former Prime Minister of the United Kingdom, was well known for her bold, occasionally obstinate leadership style. Her nickname, after all, was the "Iron Lady." That's pretty badass.

But Thatcher wasn't born made of iron. In fact, like many great public speakers throughout history, she worked with a speech coach to perfect her pitch, tone, and delivery. In the early days of her political career, Thatcher's voice was seen as too "shrill." As she practiced more and more, she lowered her pitch and perfected the steady, authoritative tone that became her hallmark.

If you've never heard Thatcher speak, look up videos of her. Then compare her voice to someone like, say, actress

Fran Drescher, or actor Gilbert Gottfried. There's no comparing the calm, high-status delivery of Thatcher to the nasally, scratchy voice of Drescher or the high-pitched, obnoxious voice of Gottfried, which we'll revisit later.

As Thatcher perfected her high-status voice over the years, her reputation as a powerful and respected leader continued to grow. If you've never given much thought or consideration to your own voice, it's time to change that.

THE POWER OF VOICE

Your vocal tonality is one of the most sincere of the honest signals. Remember when we discussed things like expensive cars and fancy handbags being dishonest signals? It's a facade that people see through. Your voice is *not* a facade. You can't fake having a high-status voice, just like you can't fake having a low-status voice.

When you have a high-status voice, people listen to you. They respect you, admire you, and, most importantly, become engaged by what you're saying. With a low-status voice, the reverse is true: people tune you out and even tend to dislike you. A lot of research shows that when people don't like the sound of someone's voice, they extrapolate that dislike to reflect their entire view of the person. Basically, instead of disliking someone's voice, we end up disliking the person. This is something that happens subconsciously. Picture someone from the opposite sex in your past that "got away." You know what I'm talking about. What if all the reasons you thought it never worked out were wrong, and the key to getting them could have been as simple as high-status vocal tonality? It's that powerful.

Everyone knows what tuning someone out looks like, right? We repeat certain phrases—*uh-huh, yep, I know, OK*. We start nodding our heads. It's an automatic pattern that we run when we're tuning someone out. We hear them, but we stop listening and just nod our heads until they shut the fuck up. That's what people do when communicating with someone with a low-status voice.

Look, we live in a digital age. Take a look around the next time you go out somewhere and just notice how many cell phones you see. It will probably shock you. Cell phones are great and all, but people are *addicted* to them. It's actually pretty scary, but for you, it's great—perfecting your high-status voice will separate you further from the cell phone addicts with low-status voices. The ability to carry on a conversation is becoming a lost art. People seem to talk in shorter sentences and phrases, maybe repeating something they saw on TV or Netflix. It's strange.

We live in a world where people can feel validation through social-media channels like Facebook and Instagram. Before the creation of all this technology, people had to, you know, actually accomplish something to gain validation. They at least had to get dressed, leave the house, and do something. Now you can get the same emotion sitting on your couch. You can take ten minutes to craft a perfect little text message, and, if it gets an *LOL* response, you feel good about yourself. You might feel better for a fleeting moment, but nothing's actually changed. You're still sitting on a couch, wondering what to do with your life or where it all went wrong. The sad but simple truth is that people avoid real-life communication.

Like all of the honest signals in this book, your vocal tonality is a skill you must practice and keep sharp. It takes practice to get it right, but this is a fantastic opportunity for you. Never has there been a greater opportunity for someone who just knows how to speak decently, not even amazingly, to stand out like ever before. For our culture, it's a bad thing, but for you personally, it's great. Take advantage of it.

SPEAKING "DOGLISH"

My girlfriend and I have two French Bulldogs. We absolutely love them, and since where we've living is close to 7,000 square feet, it's an endless oasis for these two twenty-pound dogs to explore. That's also plenty of space for them to piss and shit and, believe me, they've tagged every single room. Hey, you have to know what you're getting into when you bring puppies into the house.

After looking around online, we found this fascinating dog trainer. My friends and I call him the "Russian Dog Whisperer." One of his main training techniques is something he calls "Doglish," which is the universal language of dogs. It consists of two different vocal tonalities that dogs immediately understand and respond to. One is a high-pitched noise and the other is a deeper voice. If you've ever had a dog, you already know this. Dogs interpret high-pitched noise from a human as a reward. When you say, "Yay, good boy" in a higher pitch, a dog is going to get excited and run toward you. If you say, "No, bad dog" in a lower pitch, there's an instant physiological change in their response. The happiness disappears; they might run away and hide. They just want to get back to the high-pitched voice. This is something that's hardwired in all dogs. Every dog will respond to these two vocal tonalities. That's Doglish. Pretty fascinating, right?

HUMAN TONALITIES

Human beings really aren't that different. We are all born

with certain hardwired responses to specific tonalities, but unlike dogs, we have more than just two. For our purposes, we'll focus on three of these tonalities—seeking rapport, neutral rapport, and breaking rapport.

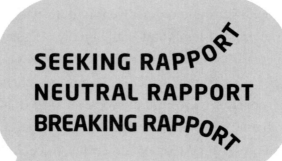

SEEKING RAPPORT

Take at a look at the vocal tonalities graphic included in this chapter. You'll see three lines moving horizontally from left to right, each one representing one of the three vocal tonalities. Seeking rapport, as it moves left to right, curves upward at the end to reflect what people do with their voices with this specific tonality.

One of the sample questions I use at my seminars to illustrate this is, "Where are you from?" When someone asks, "Where are you from?" with a seeking rapport tonality, there is an upward inflection at the end. That implies you're seeking rapport with the other person. You see their status as higher than yours and are attempting to get on their level. This signals your lower status in this interaction.

When we meet people we unconsciously view as higher status than ourselves, we speak up to them. Low-status people seek rapport with high-status people.

NEUTRAL RAPPORT

The line for neutral rapport just goes straight across. That reflects what you do with your voice in this tonality, which is completely flat. You ask, "Where are you from?" but without any intonation. This signals neutral status.

BREAKING RAPPORT

The line for this tonality curves downward at the end, opposite of seeking rapport. There is an inflection, but it's more negative. You envision that person being somewhere below you in terms of status level in that moment, so you break rapport with them. This is where the phrase "talking down to someone" comes from.

Generally speaking, I encourage everyone to stay in neutral rapport most of the time, with some breaking rapport.

FIVE TRAITS OF HIGH-STATUS VOICE

Everyone you know who has a high-status voice follows the same five traits, but they do it in their own unique way. It's the same principle as a jump shot in basketball. Every player has the same basic components—the bend at the elbow, the arc of the shot, the backspin of the ball—but they all have a slightly different way of shooting. Stephen Curry has a different form than Michael Jordan, who has a different form than Kobe Bryant. You will discover your own high-status voice.

There are two things to keep in mind before we dive into the five traits. First, your voice can be trained like a muscle. I mentioned this earlier, but it bears repeating. One of my favorite examples of this is Clark Gable, who was known as "The King of Hollywood." Not many people know this, but when he first started his career, he actually had a very high-pitched voice. It was low status, and it negatively affected his life to the point where he was almost forced to change careers. But he worked on the same things we're about to highlight in this chapter, and steadily his voice became high status. It became so high status, in fact, he ended up delivering one of the most famous movie lines of all time—"Frankly, my dear, I don't give a damn"—in *Gone with the Wind*.

Second, one of the key reasons why it's so crucial for you

to train and build your high-status voice is it will inspire others to take action. Adlai Stevenson, a famous political figure in the midtwentieth century, introduced John F. Kennedy in 1960 by saying, "Do you remember that in classical times when Cicero had finished speaking, the people would say, 'How well he spoke'; but when Demosthenes had finished speaking, they said, 'Let us march'?" That's the difference right there. A high-status voice will inspire people to action.

This will impact all walks of your life, whether at work, at home, or romantically. If you're a mother and your child doesn't listen to you, I assure you they'll pay attention to a high-status voice. If you're used to going on dates and having the other person tune out while you talk, that won't happen anymore.

Now, before we jump into the five traits of high-status voice, I need you to do one last thing: picture someone you believe has a high-status voice. It can be an actor, actress, politician, world leader, sports commentator, athlete, friend—literally anyone at all, as long as you believe they have a high-status voice. I want you to hear them in your mind and recall a time, whether it was a personal conversation, a scene in a movie, or something else, where you picked up on their unique, high-status voice. As we go through the five traits, see how they line up.

AUTHORITATIVE

A high-status voice has a certain oomph behind it. It's not hesitant and it's not questioning. Think about the person you just picked for the question above. Do they speak with authority? Of course, they do. I don't even know who you chose, but I know the answer is yes. Listen to their voice, and practice mimicking it. Not their *exact* voice—remember, you're developing your own unique voice—but practice speaking with the same tonal authority they do. It's a muscle and it needs repetitions to grow.

The other secret behind having an authoritative vocal tonality is posturing. At all of my events, I like to run people through a simple exercise to show how important posture is. First, adopt a shitty, low-status posture by sinking into your seat, hunching your back, and leaning forward. Now, imagine you're an army general and giving a speech to your troops before a battle. It's impossible to give an authoritative speech with some oomph behind it from that low-status posture.

CLEAR

The worst thing in the world to me is when someone asks me to repeat myself. It kills me. It's a signal to me that I'm not articulating clearly enough. A high-status voice is one that speaks, articulates, and enunciates clearly. Think of any great speech or presentation given throughout history. They all have a clear message and are clearly delivered.

How do you train yourself to become clearer? There are a few things to keep in mind. First, be aware. Think about it: as long as you're aware of your articulation struggles, you're not going to continue making the same mistakes. If you notice yourself not being articulate, are you just going to be like, "Well, guess I wasn't articulate today?" Bullshit, of course not. You're going to stop, restate the line, and fix it. It's called *self-correction*, and all of the most successful people in the world do it.

The second, and my personal favorite, way to train yourself is through tongue twisters. This is a fantastic way to warm up for speaking. Newscasters and sportscasters will often go through vocal warm-ups before going on-air. Once you get really good at tongue twisters, you won't have any issues speaking clearly. You can find tongue twisters online, but I've got to share a few of the ones I love. Practice these over and over and over, no matter how badly you screw them up at first or how ridiculous you think you sound.

- Whether the weather is cold, or whether the weather is hot, we'll be together whatever the weather, whether we like it or not.

- If Stew chews shoes, should Stew choose the shoes he chews?

UNAFFECTED

A study at Kent State concluded, "People unconsciously adapt to each other's voice tones, a phenomenon called communication accommodation theory." I know, that's just scientific mumbo jumbo, so here's what that really means.

When two or more people meet and have a conversation, they unconsciously adapt each other's voice tones. That's why you never see one person screaming and the other person using a very calm voice. They would be so out of rapport that they couldn't stand it.

You want to be unaffected and maintain the vocal tonality *you* want. That's what a high-status person does. You don't want to allow your emotions to impact your vocal tonality, nor do you want to seek rapport by matching someone else's vocal tonality. That's what a low-status person does.

INTERESTING

You want your vocal tonality to remain unaffected, but you don't want it to be boring. The last thing you want is to sound like monotone Ben Stein in *Ferris Bueller's Day Off*. Instead, you have to switch it up: sometimes you go bolder, other times you whisper, other times you just stay the same. It keeps things interesting and makes you more engaging.

I don't have the most subscribers on YouTube, but the company recently told me my videos do have one of the highest watch rates. People watch my videos from start to finish more than almost anyone else on all of YouTube. I attribute a lot of that to my understanding of vocal tonality.

Comedian Russell Brand has talked about vocal tonality. He's been onstage thousands of times, including sold-out shows at Madison Square Garden, and he said changing up the way you speak is one of the most important things he's learned in his career. People are constantly looking for patterns in the way people speak. Once we decipher that pattern, we basically become desensitized to it and begin to tune them out.

When you change your vocal tonality and the speed at which you speak, or the volume, you're preventing listeners from finding a pattern. They can't figure it out, so they keep listening. They remain engaged in the conversation with you, instead of tuning you out and looking elsewhere around the room. Keeping your vocal tonality interesting is a surefire way to have deeper, more meaningful conversations with friends and family.

BREAKS RAPPORT (OCCASIONALLY)

This one can be tricky. For the most part, you want your voice to remain neutral and unaffected, as we highlighted earlier. But there are certain times when a tactic known as the "status shock trick" can be effective.

You don't want to use this very often, but it's a guaranteed way to break rapport immediately and reinforce your high status. Here it is: in the middle of a conversation with someone, just yell loudly for a second. Not in a threatening way, not in a scary way, but in a fun way.

If I'm talking to someone and want to make sure I have their attention for a second, I'll just let out a "Hey!" Again, not shouting, but louder than your normal volume. It breaks your own personality and immediately reengages them. On a philological level, they go from being disengaged to immediately being alert and interested. It's a powerful shock trick that works.

COMPARING VOICES

Earlier in this chapter, I asked you to think of someone

with a high-status voice, but it's just as important to study those with low-status voices. With that in mind, this is a perfect time to revisit Gilbert Gottfried.

Gottfried's voice is incredibly high-pitched. We all know that. But if you watch him and notice his eyes and his body language, it almost looks like he's trying to break rapport. Basically, he's trying to annoy you. I don't know him personally, of course, but that's his shtick. He's low status.

On the other hand, someone like Brad Pitt consistently portrays high status. It doesn't matter what character he's playing—Rusty Ryan in *Ocean's Eleven*, Achilles in *Troy*, or John Smith in *Mr. & Mrs. Smith*. Watch him in any of his films, and you'll notice he has the same vocal traits in all of them. His vocal tonality is high status throughout.

Oprah Winfrey is another example of someone with a high-status voice. She is authoritative, she is clear, her vocal tonality changes, and she occasionally breaks rapport. She's got it down. Lena Dunham, by comparison, has a low-status voice. It has a whiny, acerbic tone that isn't authoritative, doesn't change tone, and isn't overly articulate. Comparing Oprah and Dunham is like comparing the sun to a lightbulb. It's not even close.

THE IMPORTANCE OF TIMING

When Dean Martin and Frank Sinatra used to perform in Las Vegas, people would typically admire Sinatra as he sang. But when he made jokes, they wouldn't laugh. Martin, on the other hand, drew laughs every time he told a joke. People would even laugh when he just walked onstage. Martin understood physical humor, and he understood timing.

One day, Sinatra was fed up. He told Martin before they went onstage that he wanted to do the funny lines for once. Martin agreed to switch lines that night, but it didn't matter. The audience was still laughing at Martin, who was supposed to be playing the straight man, not the funny guy. At one point, Sinatra got so frustrated he broke the scene onstage and said, "Why the hell is no one laughing at me right now?" Martin, without missing a beat, shot back, "Because you're not funny." Perfect timing. The entire audience erupted into laughter. This is also a prime example of high-status truth, which we'll explore later on.

A lot of people don't understand timing, but it's a crucial component of a high-status voice. When we meet someone who's polished but authentic, and passionate but controlled as a speaker, we identify them as high status. The people who are great at communicating usually rise to the top of their industry. That's just the way it is.

BUILDING YOUR VOICE

Demosthenes is one of the most famous orators in the history of ancient Greece, but like everyone who has ever been great at something, he wasn't born like that. In fact, he had a speech impediment as a child. He didn't care: he wanted to become a great speaker. He dedicated himself to overcoming his impediment, and that often involved some unorthodox methods.

At one point, he shaved half of his head, so he'd be afraid to go out in public. Instead, it forced him to stay inside and practice speaking all day. He would also practice speaking with pebbles in his mouth to better train his voice. Don't worry—you're not going to have to do either of those practices. It's just another illustration that your voice, like any muscle, can be trained. Demosthenes went from a boy with a speech impediment to one of the classical figures we remember during that period in history, along with the likes of Caesar, Cicero, and Mark Antony.

Here are a few practices to work on that don't involve shaving your head or holding rocks in your mouth.

TAKE DEEP BREATHS

When you start to run low on oxygen in your diaphragm, your vocal tonality will shut down. It becomes weaker, parched, and flimsy. But when you take a full breath of air and really fill your lungs up, your voice becomes stronger.

What I have a lot of my clients do at my events is come up onstage and talk for as long as they can without taking an inhalation. I have everyone start by saying, "I love being high status because..." and they take it from there. For those first ten to fifteen seconds, everyone starts off strong. Eventually, their voices trail off, getting weaker and weaker until they have to stop to take a breath.

We run them through it again, except this time I tell them to pause and take a good inhalation as they begin. Slow down and take a few deep breaths. You notice the difference immediately. Your voice is strong, authoritative, and doesn't trail off.

TURN UP THE VOLUME

No, don't go around yelling at everyone. Just turn the volume of your voice up by 20 percent. That's it. People who express themselves loudly are typically seen as higher status. This is something you'll have to work on, but remember, your voice is a muscle. It's all part of the training.

Here's how we do it. First, start carrying a book around

with you. It can be a physical book or an e-book saved on your phone: it doesn't matter as long as you have access to it. Practice reading one page of the book at 20 percent higher volume than you normally would. Do this three times a day, once in the morning, once in the afternoon, and once at night. By the second day, you'll find yourself speaking louder. If you want to be ambitious, repeat this exercise for a full seven days, and then one day per week after that, to keep the muscle strong.

The second exercise is similar to the first, but instead of speaking 20 percent louder while reading a book, you're going to speak 20 percent louder in every conversation you have during that day. You'll notice the difference in how people respond to you right away. The more you practice this, the more natural it will become.

If you're thinking, "Jason, sounds great, but how do I know what's 20 percent louder than my usual voice?" Don't worry. Think about the volume of your voice on a scale of 1 to 10, with 10 being the loudest. What do you normally speak at? Most people that answer this question say a 5 or 6. If you think you're at a 5 usually, bump it up to a 7.

The best thing you can do, regardless of the situation, is just relax and take a few deep breaths before you start speaking. If you're worried about an upcoming situation that's going to be stressful, practice the right tonality in your head. We all self-talk: there's a voice inside all of our heads. Just rehearse it mentally first, then out loud a few times. It will get easier and more natural with practice.

Virtually everything we cover in this book will become more instinctive as you continue to practice, until you reach the point where you don't think about it anymore. You will just naturally *be* high status. It will become your new "default setting," and all the perks, prizes and benefits that come along with it will be yours as well. And recognize this: you already know more than most people on what it means to be a truly high-status person. But in our next chapter, we are going to cover arguably the *most* important honest signal of high status in the game. You are going to love this one. Keep reading.

Chapter Five

HIGH-STATUS EYE CONTACT

———

Men lie, women lie, shiny shit lies. People lie all the time with what they say and how they present themselves, but there's one part of our bodies that doesn't allow lies—the eyes. It is *impossible* for the eyes to lie about status. Eyes are the most important honest signal, and it all comes down to just two things that will convey your status level. These are things no one has ever talked about or told you, because they're a result of my own empirical data from years and years of research. High-status eye contact comes down to attention and tension. That's it.

High-status eye contact can get you just about anything in this world. On the flip side, low-status eye contact will ensure you come out on the short end of deals and constantly miss out on things you want. If you understand how to use attention with your eyes, and harness tension both within yourself and others, you can have the highest-status eye contact in the entire world. We're going to tackle both of these shortly, but first, a quick story.

I was recently in Las Vegas with my girlfriend and a few of my buddies. I don't party as often as I did when I was younger, but when I do, I fucking *party*. That's always true when we hit up Vegas. We're out there having a great time, sharing some drinks at a club, but it was just a precursor for the main event—Drai's After Hours. All of us in the group love house music and Drai's always plays it.

As the night's progressing and it's getting closer to 2:00 a.m.—when Drai's opens—I asked my buddy John if he wanted to head over before us and grab some tables. That way, we wouldn't have to waste any time waiting in line. We were in Vegas to party, not stand around waiting. John was all about it. "I got it, don't even worry about it."

It hits 2:00 a.m. and we show up at Drai's. The line to get in is massive, but we walk straight to the front because I saw John waiting with the general manager of the club. I had met him once before, so I knew his name was Mark, but inside I'm thinking, "Why the hell is John with the owner? And why the hell is the owner even here?"

As I'm wondering what the hell is about to happen, the owner walks up to me and says, "Jason, we're so glad to have you here. Thank you so much for coming. Come on guys, follow me." OK, interesting turn. I figured I was about to get one hell of a story from John once we got inside.

Drai's is an incredible place. I highly recommend you check it out if you can. The nightclub is underground, so you've got to take an elevator down. When the doors open, you walk right out into the club, a massive room with red walls and leather furniture and a bass-heavy sound system that shakes you to your core. It's sick. Well, normally it is. That night it was quiet and empty as Mark walked us in.

As we sat down at our table, Mark started explaining the situation to me. "As John might have told you, Drai's is now split into two clubs—the hip-hop room and the house room. It's Sunday night, so the house room is closed, unfortunately. But I talked to John about it and he told me your preferences, so we decided to open the house room up for you guys. Your own security guard, your own waitress, your own DJ. Just you and your group. Is that OK with you?"

Um, let me think...*fuck yes*. How cool was that? It turned into a great night, one of those memorable times we all still talk about it now. So, how did my buddy John make it happen? Eye contact.

When John got to Drai's, the bouncer told him about the house room being closed for the night. "Sorry man, we only have hip-hop tonight." Rather than just accept that, turn tail, and leave, John remembered what I had taught him about high-status eye contact. Instead of saying anything else to the bouncer, he just looked at him in a very specific, high-status way. After about five seconds passed, the bouncer said he'd go talk to the manager.

The manager then came over and told John the same exact thing. And again, John responded the same way. He let out a deep exhale, like he was disappointed, and held the same high-status eye contact with the manager. Another five seconds went by before the manager said, "You know what? I might be able to do something. Let me go talk to the owner."

A few minutes later, Mark comes over. "What is it you wanted to do?" he asks. John then explains that his "client" will be arriving soon with a big group of people and will be disappointed that the house room is closed. John held the high-status eye contact one more time, and after a short conversation with the manager, came back with the plan.

I love John. He's a great guy and one of my best friends, but he's not extraordinarily handsome, he's not rich, and he's not the best-dressed guy in the world. None of those traits played a factor in his ability to get a private club at Drai's. It was all about eye contact.

ATTENTION

Your eyes communicate to everyone else where your attention is at that moment. If you walk into a room and someone is sitting on a couch watching TV, you instantly know their attention is on the TV screen. As human beings, we're hardwired to recognize things that are abundant and easy to obtain as having less value than things that are scarce. This logic doesn't just apply to physical objects.

If your attention is easily had by anyone at any time, are you more or less valuable? You're less valuable. If your attention is harder to get, that makes it more valuable. The harder your attention is to get, the higher your status. Think about it. If you're working on something that's a priority on your path to your high-status destiny, and someone asks you to grab dinner, you don't just immediately drop everything and follow them. If you do, you're indicating that your destiny isn't the most important thing to you. That's low status.

Instead, you remain focused on the task at hand. You don't have to ignore the dinner request, but say you need another ten or twenty minutes. Can you imagine if the President of the United States was working on a crucial negotiation with a foreign prime minister, but ended the meeting as soon as his dinner was ready? Fuck no, of course not. The President is a high-status person, so dinner is going to have to wait.

TENSION

Tension has a terrible connotation, doesn't it? But guess what? Tension doesn't have to be a bad thing. What happens when most people feel tension? All of their other high-status signals go to shit. They become fidgety, their posture suffers, their vocal pace and tone gets thrown off. They're just trying to end the tension as quickly as possible.

High-status people are able to bask in tension like they're kicking back on a warm, sunny day at the beach, watching the waves drift in and out. That's how comfortable they are in high-tension situations. When you can stay relaxed in the midst of tension, you are signaling to others that you are a high-status person.

When John made his request to the three different guys at Drai's, those were obviously tension-filled moments, but he was able to bask in the tension, instead of folding under it. Unconsciously, those guys were sizing him up by saying to themselves, "I don't know who his client is, but he must be a big deal because he's so relaxed right now. He looks like he makes these type of requests all the time, and he looks like he's used to hearing 'yes,' so I should probably say 'yes' too."

THE POWER OF EYE CONTACT

John's story is a great example of the power that high-status eye contact has, but there are countless other examples. High-status people know how to look at the eyes of someone and almost entrance them in a powerful, positive, and uplifting way. One of the all-time best at this was Frank Sinatra.

Think about how many people throughout history have had blue eyes. Too many to count, right? Well, there's only one "Frankie Blue Eyes," so that alone says something. His valet, George Jacobs, wrote, "When he would train those hypnotic eyes on her or anyone else, there was a magic moment when that woman was the woman, the only woman, and that was irresistible to them."

More examples of this come from *Fifty Shades of Grey*. It might not be the greatest book ever written, but shit, it's sold more than 120 million copies. As someone who used to be a dating coach, I've read it a few times to study why Christian Grey is so alluring to women. Throughout the book, there is commentary after commentary, quote after quote, talking only about his eye contact from the perspective of Ana Steele. For example: "Jose and Christian, they both want something from me. Jose is easy to deal with, but Christian? Christian takes a whole different league of handling of understanding. Part of me wants to run and hide. What am I going to do? His burning gray eyes and that intense smoldering stare come into my mind's eye and my body tightens at the thought. I gasp. He's not even here and I'm turned on." Boom—all about the eyes. Here are a few more:

- "His gaze is unwavering and intense."
- "'I've never introduced a woman to my mother before. What are you doing to me?' His eyes burned. Their intensity takes my breath away."
- "He gazes down at me and his eyes are heated, lustful, hypnotic. His gaze is so intense I nod, my mouth dry, my heart feeling as if it would jump out of my chest."

You get the point, but this further emphasizes how important—and powerful—eye contact can be. It's something you will have to master for all situations, regardless of whether it's just a friendly conversation with the cashier at Chipotle or your first time being intimate with a new partner. Eye contact is crucial in high-stakes situations, like a potential job interview or important meeting. When there's deep, powerful eye contact between two people, it just screams higher status.

RULES OF HIGH-STATUS EYE CONTACT

High-status eye contact is strong and powerful, but also relaxed. Someone with high-status eye contact looks where they want to look. They're not looking where other people want them to look. They're not sheep. It's like being an audience member at a late-night talk show, but not automatically laughing when the producer flashes the "laugh" sign. If you're in the middle of a conversation with a friend, and you're giving them your attention, you won't just abandon it when there's some commotion off to the side. As a high-status person, your attention must go where you *want* it to go.

Eye contact has to be trained for two distinct purposes—attention, which is on the outside, and tension, which is on the inside. There are a few different techniques to do this.

80/60 RULE

When you're talking to someone, you want to be looking them in the eyes about 80 percent of the time. This isn't a hard-and-fast rule. It's more of a general idea to give you a frame of reference. When they are speaking to you, you want to be looking them in the eyes only about 60 percent of the time.

Why is this? Well, when you're looking them dead in the eyes, you're signaling that you're not only important, but also confident enough to communicate with them. When they're speaking, you're signaling that your attention is just a bit harder to come by. All you have to do is pull back a little bit—remember, when in doubt, lean out—and glance to the left or right a few times. The other person will pick up on this and push harder to gain your attention.

COMMUNICATE VISION WITH YOUR EYES

When Steve Jobs would describe the iPod to someone before it was created, he would maintain eye contact with them until he arrived a really big, emotional part of the discussion. At that point, instead of maintaining eye contact, he would look down at his hands and imagine he was holding an iPod. He would move his thumb in a circular motion to show the motion wheel, or swipe his finger up and down to convey a different motion.

The other person might have absolutely no fucking idea what he was talking about, but they couldn't deny his passion. He appeared powerful and excited about life—in other words, high status. Jobs could communicate that passion through his eyes.

SLOW HEAD TURN

I've used this example already, but fuck it, I absolutely love Robert Downey Jr.'s portrayal of Tony Stark in the *Iron Man* and *Avengers* movies. When he's down in his lab working on a new machine, and Pepper Potts asks if she can talk to him, he doesn't immediately drop what he's doing and look up.

What he's working on is incredibly important: it's his high-status destiny. Instead, he'll focus for a few seconds and then start slowly turning his head to deviate some of his attention away from his project. It's an extremely high-status move.

SINGULAR FOCUS EXERCISE

This exercise is specifically for training tension. You'll need a few things for this. First, a computer. Any laptop works, as long as it can play videos. Pick a video, mute it, and hit play. We only need the visual for this exercise.

Next, set something taller behind the computer screen that you can see, such as a flower vase or book.

For thirty seconds, pick a spot on the object behind the screen and, in a relaxed way, just focus on it as the video plays. After a few seconds, you'll notice your focus and concentration starting to drift. Maybe the video will catch your attention or something else in the room. When that starts to happen, calmly recite the following to yourself: recognize and return.

Recognize that your attention is fading, and return it to the spot you chose to focus on. Don't get mad or frustrated with yourself. Try this a couple times for thirty seconds, and then eventually build up to ninety seconds and two minutes. If you get to the point where you can do this for two minutes and only have to recognize and return a handful of times, you'll be in the top 1 percent in the world in your ability to focus on something. That ability to stay focused will keep you relaxed and focused when facing tension.

COLD SHOWER

If you've ever taken a cold shower, you know how shitty it is. I don't need to take the time to explain it. But in terms of using external forces to put your body and mind in a high-tension situation, there aren't many better methods.

When you step into the shower and that cold water hits your skin, it's a shock to the system. You tense up, your muscles tighten, and you might squeeze your fists together. What's going on internally is that your body is recognizing that as a high-tension situation.

What I want you to do is take a cold shower, but stay *relaxed*. Remember, a high-status person embraces tension. When that cold water hits you, don't freak out. Let it run over you for just twenty seconds. Start small, even though the first time will feel like eternity. Don't clench your jaw, and try to keep your muscles as relaxed as possible.

The next time you do this, increase it to thirty seconds, then forty-five. Get all the way up to two minutes if you can. Trust me, if you can stand two minutes of ice-cold water hitting every inch of your naked body and you remain relaxed, there is nothing in the world that can throw you off balance.

AM I GOING TO DIE?

I can't stress this enough: eye contact is the No. 1 honest signal. It's crucial to achieving high status. I'll leave you with two more things before we close out this chapter.

I get asked a lot of the same questions at my seminars. This is one I regularly hear: "I'm relaxed and holding eye contact with a person, but what if the tension just gets to be too much? What if I can't take it?" There are a few options here. First, ask yourself a simple question in your mind: am I going to die? Of course, the answer is no, right? Once you remind yourself that you're not going to die from looking at someone, it puts things in perspective. It allows you to hold the eye contact for a few more seconds.

Another tactic to combat tension is a simple thought loop. If you're feeling the tension of the moment, and in your mind, you're thinking, "I can't take this, I can't take this," then you're not going to be able to take it. Change that thought loop from "I can't take this" to "I love myself." Just repeat that to yourself a few times in that situation, and pay attention to how quickly the tension gives way to calmness. It's amazing how effectively a simple thought loop helps us find peace of mind.

It's further proof that you really are the one in control. You're attacking your destiny, and you're in control of your body language, voice, and eye contact. You are becoming more and more high status with every new word you read in this book. This is a great place to be, but there's still much more to discover, starting now with your high-status walk.

Chapter Six

HIGH-STATUS WALK

———

Not long ago I was driving from my house to a local hotel for one of my private workshops. It was a beautiful, late-summer day in California. The sun was shining and I could feel a nice breeze against my skin with the top of the car down. It was just a gorgeous day.

The hotel was located in a central area of Orange County full of corporate-looking buildings. As I sat at a red light at an intersection, I noticed three guys from the nine-to-five office crowd waiting to cross the street in front of me. How did I know they were office drones? Easy—they were each wearing a wrinkled button-up shirt with a cheap tie and khakis. Not only that, but they were standing there, taking bites of their Subway sandwiches. They were rushed, uncomfortable, and unhappy: they were low status.

You could just tell they were trying to eat as quickly as possible on their walk back to the office. Eventually, they got the green light to cross the intersection, and at that point their nervous standing gave way to a rushed, fidgety walk. At the same time, a strong gust of wind blew through the intersection, and I watched as pieces of lettuce from all three sandwiches simultaneously blew away. I immediately dubbed the hapless trio the "sandwich brigade," but it's not just a California phenomenon: there are people like this at every street corner in every city.

It was the saddest image I have ever seen in my life. Ever. The ancestors of those three men used to slay animals, protect their families, and build shelters, but they couldn't even get their clothing straight, find the time to finish a sandwich, or find a job that makes them comfortable. What the fuck is going on?

As I made the left turn and continued on my way to the hotel, the image of those three guys was burned into my mind. The workshop was for entrepreneurs, so I had planned to discuss the finer techniques of being a self-starter. Instead, I spent the first twenty minutes sharing the same story with the fifty or so people in the workshop. Some laughed, some nodded their heads, but everyone agreed it was a sad example. It's amazing how much is conveyed through people's subcommunications.

THE POWER OF YOUR WALK

There's a distinct difference between a high-status walk and a low-status walk. A high-status walk carries a lot more power with it. There are literally countless examples of high-status walks throughout history, but one of my favorite examples is Marlon Brando.

When Mary Tyler Moore was still in the early stages of her career, she had a series of small roles in movies. She was involved in a Marlon Brando movie at the peak of his popularity, when he was arguably the most famous actor on the planet. She was hanging out on the set one day with a number of her friends when they all saw Brando for the first time. He was only walking the short distance from the stage to his trailer, but it mesmerized Moore and her entire group. How could he do that without even looking in their direction? His walk, of course.

Brando didn't look left or right as he walked to his trailer. He didn't say or do anything. He didn't have to. He just had a unique, high-status walk. Moore said in that moment that Brando had the slowest, sexiest walk she had ever seen. Decades later, she said the image of Brando walking to his trailer was still the sexiest walk she had ever seen in her entire life. It was burned into her memory, the same way the sad image of the "sandwich brigade" is burned into mine. The lesson here? People will conclude a lot about you from the way you walk. Walking is something we all do, and, like all of the honest signals, it can't be faked.

Think of anyone you believe exhibits a high-status walk. It can be Marlon Brando, Brad Pitt, Daniel Craig, Adriana Lima, Beyoncé, Kim Kardashian—anyone at all. The most important thing to remember is every single person you know with a high-status walk has their own unique style. There are five traits that are universal to high-status walk, but everyone has a different personal style. Your high-status walk will be exclusive to you.

The first thing you'll want to do is start observing people's walks. Just by reading this book you've already started to gain awareness about something most people would never even think about. As you watch other people, decide whether their walk is high or low status. If it's high status, what made you draw that conclusion? Airports are a phenomenal place to study this, because *everyone* is walking. If you take a second to notice how someone is walking, you'll be able to pick up on whether they're excited or unhappy. Someone that's about to take a week-long vacation to Aruba is going to be looking ahead and walking with a strong posture and purpose. The person who's being sent to the middle of nowhere for a shitty business meeting they have no interest in will have a slow, distracted walk. Trust me, next time you're in an airport, remember this chapter.

FIVE TRAITS OF HIGH-STATUS WALK

Though everyone has their own unique walk, there are five traits that are found in every high-status walk. Let's break them all down:

TALL AND OPEN

This means exactly what it sounds like—good posture, shoulders back, eyes looking straight ahead, chin up. Imagine there's a string that begins at your lower back, and comes straight up and attaches to the back of your neck and crown of your head. The string extends toward the ceiling, essentially pulling you up.

Imagine what that would look like. That's what it means to walk tall and open. Simple.

PURPOSEFUL

A high-status walk knows where it's going. It has direction; it has a destination in mind; it has purpose. Again, a person at the airport who is about to board a flight to Aruba for vacation is going to have a different walk than someone about to board a flight to Pittsburgh for a work meeting. No offense, Pittsburgh, but people would much rather go to Aruba.

Think about characters who portray high status in movies or TV shows. They are almost never shown conversing, while sitting down doing nothing. They're always walking down a hallway because they have somewhere to be. Their walks are purposeful.

The exact opposite of this is when people get to a bar or club and decide to "take a lap." Maybe they don't know anyone there, or they don't know where to go, so they walk around. It's completely purposeless. It broadcasts to everyone else, "Hey, I don't know anyone here, but I want to meet someone." It comes off low status. Don't do laps. Have a purpose to your walk.

SMOOTH AND CONTROLLED

Remember how one of the five traits of a high-status voice is that it remains unaffected by others? Well, the same is true of a high-status walk. A high-status voice speaks the way it wants to, and a high-status walk moves at the pace it wants to.

When I used to live in Marina del Rey, I would walk around

a lot. I didn't have a car, but I didn't need one. Everything I needed was within walking distance, plus the traffic was fucking brutal. Nowhere was that more true than Lincoln Boulevard. It's one of the more famous streets in Los Angeles, where Venice, Santa Monica, and Marina del Rey all touch each other. The traffic and crowded intersections were shitty for drivers, but it gave me a perfect training area to perfect my own high-status walk.

When the walk light would turn green, instead of sprinting across the crosswalk like the sandwich brigade, I would take a deep breath, wait a second, and then start walking. It was purposeful and at my own pace. By the time I was 20 percent across the street, everyone else had already crossed. I didn't care. I walked a smooth, controlled pace. I would only get about 75 percent of the way across the street before the light turned red, so I'm sure I pissed off many, many drivers.

I'm not encouraging you to go out and piss off every driver in your city, but walking across streets at intersections is a great way to practice a smooth and controlled walk.

CASUALLY SEXY

Add just a teaspoon of sexy to your walk. Add a little swagger, but don't go overboard. There's a fine line between sexiness and overexaggeration. Subtlety is sexy.

Imagine there's a camera on you as you walk, and on the other side of the camera is every person you find attractive. They're all watching you—the way you move, the way you walk. It's your big moment. What do you do? Just add a teaspoon of sexy to your walk. Too much salt kills the dish, so don't overdo it. Take your time, keep it smooth and controlled.

LOOK BEYOND THE CROWD

This one is key. A person with a high-status walk is looking beyond the crowd toward their vision—their destiny. Their head isn't on a swivel. They aren't looking left or right, and they aren't taken off their path by every little distraction. A high-status person is in control of their attention, because their attention is valuable.

After one of my coaching groups met together, we went to great restaurant called Meze Greek Fusion. Side note: this place has the best saganaki I've ever had. Anyway, we're all there eating, drinking, having a good time. There was a belly dancer going around table to table trying to teach people how to belly dance. When she eventually came over to our table, I was in the middle of a really focused conversation with my friend. When I'm having a conversation with someone, I'm present. I'm not looking around for other distractions or outside stimulation. Neither of us looked up as she tried, repeatedly, to get our attention. At one point, she even hit the table to get us to look up, but we didn't. We were both peripherally aware of her, but learning how to belly dance just wasn't important. Being present with a good friend of mine was.

If you can walk straight and look straight ahead through all the bullshit, be excited about where you're going, walk tall and open, smooth and controlled, all with a hint of sexiness, that's high-status walk at its peak.

I want you to start internalizing your own unique high-status walk today. Don't put this off, and I'll tell you why. Remember *Willy Wonka & the Chocolate Factory*? The one with Gene Wilder, not the weird remake with Johnny Depp. One of the most memorable and classic scenes from that movie is the first time we see Willy Wonka. No one has seen him in years, but the five golden-ticket holders are among the hundreds of people waiting at the front gate. When he finally comes out to greet them, he's using a cane and limping because of a bad leg. A hush falls over the crowd—that's not who they were expecting to see. Suddenly, he drops the cane, does a somersault, and everyone goes crazy. It's a fantastic scene.

Here's the thing: one day *you* could be Willy Wonka. Not the jovial, joking Wonka, but the broken-down, cane-wielding Wonka. You only have a limited amount of time where you're able to walk the Earth in a genuinely high-status way. Do not wait.

ENTERING ROOMS

Aristotle famously said the brains of human beings are teleological, which means that we are goal seeking. Our brains thrive on goals. Viktor Frankl wrote *Man's Search for Meaning*, which chronicled his time as a concentration camp inmate at Auschwitz during the Holocaust. It's an amazing book that describes how he not only survived, but made a difference and affected so many people later in life. He turned an absolutely horrifying experience into a long-term positive by realizing his purpose. Frankl would use the experience as a way to teach others that they can survive anything.

Frankl had given his brain a goal, and when our brains have goals, we're much happier. The size of the goal doesn't matter. It can be as grand as discovering your life's purpose, as Frankl did, or it can be as seemingly unimportant as entering a room.

If you can say to yourself, "This is why I'm here, and this

is what I'm going to do," before entering a room, you will give yourself a quick little goal. It's teleological, and it's better than entering a room with no goal.

PAUSE AT THE DOOR

Most people scurry into rooms like rats. When a rat is trying to get into or out of a room, it will just dart in and out. It doesn't want to be seen. A high-status person isn't like that.

A high-status person pauses for a second in the doorway. They're entering a new environment, so they want to take it in. Who are the movers and shakers? Who are the key players in this room? Who are the high-status people here? Do I know anyone? A slight pause in the doorway allows you to read the room.

BREATHE IN THE ROOM

While you pause at the door, take a deep breath, and breathe the room in. Set your intention as you exhale. Why are you there? What are you going to do? What do you hope to accomplish? What kind of person do you want to be in this room?

Most people enter a room with no direction or purpose.

They're just kind of...there. Don't just be there. Don't float around. High-status people know where they are there.

BECOME THE FOCUS

Step 3 is actually more of a benefit than anything. Steps 1 and 2 will only take a total of somewhere between five and ten seconds, but it's amazing how quickly you will become the focus of that room. People will turn to look at you. You will immediately be recognized as high status. It's instant and it's powerful.

WORKING ON YOUR WALK

OK, so we've established the five traits of high-status walk—tall and open, purposeful, smooth and controlled, casually sexy, and looking beyond the crowd. Remember these, review them, and reread this section as often as you need. You'll need to keep them in mind for the next steps.

First, identify a high-status walk that you love. Make sure it's someone that you can study, whether in movies, TV shows, or online. You've got to be able to consistently access video footage of them walking. It's funny. A lot of times when I work with people on their walk, they'll say, "Jason, this isn't my natural walk." My follow-up question is always, "How do you know to walk the way you walk?"

It stumps everyone, but the answer is simple. Like many actions and habits, we picked it up as a child and never changed it. This is now your chance to change your walk for the better. Make it a good one.

Second, start practicing power walks. Another term for this is a *walk of fame*. It's the opposite of a walk of shame—leaving in the morning while wearing last night's clothes, nursing a hangover from a full night of bad decisions. There's a shameful vibe and it's nearly impossible to have a high-status walk in that situation. A walk of fame, on the other hand, is all about high status. Imagine you've been searching for your pot of gold for decades and you've finally found it, or you're an actor or actress and have finally landed your first starring role. Picture any similar scenario where you've accomplished a goal in your high-status destiny. How will your walk look? That's your walk of fame. There are three steps to training for this:

REVIEW THE FIVE TRAITS

I can't stress this enough. Review the section on the five traits of a high-status walk over and over, until you feel comfortable. Luckily, they're written permanently in ink in this book, so you can review them anytime.

WATCH YOUR MODEL

Once you've reviewed the traits, go to your computer or TV, and watch the person you selected earlier as your model. Watch them for one minute, ideally in a scene where they're walking.

PRACTICE, PRACTICE, PRACTICE

You've reviewed the five traits and watched your high-status walk model in action. Now, practice modeling their walk for one minute. You can do this outside, in your apartment, wherever. Do this process three times in a row. It shouldn't take longer than ten minutes from start to finish.

Repeat this formula for a full week. Your brain will not only become focused on the five specific traits, but it will have an image for reference from your model. By the end of the week, your walk will have completely and effortlessly transformed forever.

PERFECTING YOUR WALK

Before we wrap up this chapter on the high-status walk, there are a few more quick tips to keep in mind. One thing I always tell my clients is to be aware of how you walk first thing in the morning. That first walk of the day sets the tone, so when you get out of bed to go to the bathroom, brush your teeth, or make some coffee, just be aware of how you walk. Remember the traits, remember what your high-status walk looks like, and jump right into it.

I've found that it's typically easier to start practicing your high-status walk in new environments. If you're in a new city, building, or place where no one really knows you, it's definitely easier than a normal environment, surrounded by friends and family. All it takes is one person to make a comment about your new walk to cast some doubt. Don't let that shit happen! If someone says something to you, like, "Hey, you're walking different," just look at them and respond, "Yeah, I feel great, thanks."

I have my clients practice a simple thought loop when they're practicing their high-status walk. When walking, simply say to yourself, "God, I am spectacular." Very simple, right? Walk tall, walk relaxed—God, I am spectacular. It might even make you chuckle a bit, which is great. You want to be relaxed and light. Trust me, if you repeat that to yourself a few times, before you know it you'll be in motion.

If you ever feel like you're too jerky in your walk or not relaxed enough, just take a deep breath and slow it down. Practice makes perfect, so practice as much as you can.

It's natural to want to get to a point where it doesn't feel weird anymore. You will get there, trust me.

If you complete the weeklong, power walk exercise, it will feel natural by the end of the week. At that point, you won't have to think about it anymore. A high-status walk will be ingrained in your subconscious. Look at it this way: we walk *everywhere*, so you might as well get really good at it.

That's actually true for all twelve of the honest signals, including the next one—and it's a big one—state control. So many people come to me because they recognize that they are missing opportunity after opportunity in life because they let their emotions control them, instead of them controlling their emotions. Make no mistake, emotions make a terrific servant but a tyrannical master. We must master our emotions instead of letting them master us, if we are to win our own game of life. And guess what? It's easy! I'll show you right now how simple it is.

Chapter Seven

HIGH-STATUS STATE CONTROL

———

What exactly is state control? As a girl at an event once asked me, is it being in control of Hawaii, Nevada, Wyoming, or any of the other forty-seven states in America? Of course not. State is your mood, how you feel in a given moment. State control is the mastering of your emotions so that you consistently feel positive, and not down, hopeless, or stuck. By practicing state control, you will learn how to remain unaffected by external distractions, so that your mood is dependent upon only yourself and nothing else. Not on the weather, the food you ate, or the workload you have. You don't allow externalities to impact your state. Who likes feeling like shit? No one. State control allows *you* to take control of your emotions and choose how you feel.

The state you are in most often becomes your default setting. This makes sense, right? If you're consistently putting yourself in a good mood, that will become the state you go to sleep in at night and wake up in. There are six specific practices to build your high-status state control, but before we dive into them, I want to share a personal story that illustrates my own maturity and understanding when it comes to state control.

A few years ago, my company was in the middle of its biggest promotion of the year for all customers world-wide. We had built up the promotion the entire previous week by sending out different e-mails and videos and blog posts. It was a big day, both for the company and for me personally. The day finally arrived and, of course, the e-mail server crashed. There was no way for us to send out the promotion, and worse, no way to let subscribers know why they weren't getting it. At that point, I was still in control of my state, so I started focusing on ways to work around the problem. If we could move all of the necessary information over to another server within a few hours, we could temporarily use that second server until the main one was up and running again.

I contacted another e-mail service provider to register an account with them, only to find out their server had also crashed. OK, what are the chances? But I was still in control of my state. I go to a third provider. They had also crashed. Fourth provider, same story. At that point, my state took a tumble. I felt like I was out of options and accepted defeat. It was so bad that, for the first time in years, I drove to a liquor store, bought a bottle of vodka, and finished half of the damn thing by 4:00 p.m. I was brewing. I was angry. I had lost control of my state. We got everything straightened out two days later, but the damage was done. It was a shitty experience.

A similar situation happened more recently. Once again, we had a big promotion that we were gearing up for, but when I logged into the e-mail service provider, it wasn't working. It turned out the provider had actually shut us down because they didn't like the content from an e-mail the previous week. I had mentioned a famous celebrity's name in the e-mail, and the service provider flagged it for spamming. I'm friends with the aforementioned celebrity, but the provider didn't take the time to verify that, so whatever. It's water under the bridge at this point.

Unlike the first e-mail-server fiasco from a few years before, I stayed in total control of my state. I hopped on Facebook and wrote up a short post to my customers explaining the situation and asking if they'd be so kind to e-mail the service provider. Within an hour, they got over 300 e-mails. Team Capital fucking rocks. An hour later, my account was turned back on, and I got a direct call from the provider's vice president.

Your ability to control your state in the stressful and unexpected situations that life will inevitably throw at you is critically important.

YOU ARE IN CONTROL

Allow me a moment of locker-room talk, if you will. There was a point in my life where I was the king of taking home the second-hottest girl in the bar. It's not exactly a title that rolls off the tongue, but it described me perfectly. I had trouble talking to anyone I felt was the most beautiful girl in a bar or club. I spent a lot of time trying to figure out why that was, and what was holding me back. Eventually, I realized I was attributing so much significance to these women and giving them so much control over my emotions that it made me nervous. I wasn't in control of my state around them.

One night I was out with my friends, and as I was mapping the room based on the women there—all guys do this, whether they admit it or not—I noticed one in particular. She had long blonde hair and was wearing a florescent lime green dress. She was just this orb of attractive, shiny light, and she was one of the most beautiful girls I had seen in a long time. At one point, I noticed her at the bar, with her friends off to one side. I decided to go for it.

Most guys in that situation would approach her and immediately start talking to her. But that's a pattern she's used to, and it's not what I did. I went up to the bar, right next to her, but I kept my eyes forward. Eventually, she said something like, "The bartender's not giving us any attention over here."

I looked at her and replied, "Yeah, you know, you're right. In fact, why don't you tell me what kind of drink you want to buy me?"

Her expression evolved from surprised anger to a curious smirk, like she was thinking, "Who is this guy?"

She stared me down for a second, and on the inside, I was nervous as shit. But on the outside, I was mindful of my state control. Whether or not it was going to work, it was still a great opportunity to practice my ability to hold my state and be the sole determinant of how I was going to feel. After a few seconds, she answered.

"Is that your pickup line?"

Shit, that's the heavy artillery. If a girl wants to shoot a guy down, she'll usually drop the "I appreciate you coming over to talk, but I'm not interested" or "I have a boyfriend." This was clearly a test. I looked back at her and held my smirk. If she let two seconds pass, I let three seconds pass.

"Yes, and I would like a shot of Patrón. Thank you," I finally said. Then I turned and started talking to someone on my left. Not a minute later, I felt a tap on my shoulder. It was her, and she was holding drinks for both of us. We took the shots and spent the rest of the night getting to know each other. That was a major moment of awakening for me. She later told me the thing that attracted her to me most was that I didn't flinch. I didn't back down. I was a strong male in a world full of weak males, and she wasn't used to that.

LIES ABOUT YOUR STATE

People typically allow externalities—things that are out of their control—to dictate their state. It's like a professional athlete relying on cheers and praise from fans to affect their state in a positive way. That sounds great in the moment, but eventually that athlete will become a victim of their externalities. The minute those fans turn on them, what happens? The player can lose focus, their confidence can suffer, and they can even feel anger toward the fans. In that situation, they have no control over their own state. The fans do.

Fans should never determine how a player feels about themselves. Likewise, external factors should not affect your mood. You should be the sole determinant. Knowing this, why is it that most people allow externalities to dictate their state? We've all been fed a few different lies when it comes to our state.

LIE NO. 1: YOU'RE ALONG FOR THE RIDE

There's this idea that permeates our society that how you feel in a given moment is, quite simply, out of your control. You might feel happy or sad or angry, but it's because other things have caused those states. It's complete bullshit.

To prove how ridiculous this logic is, I like to utilize a simple technique at many of my seminars. I'll ask everyone in attendance to write down how they feel on a scale of 1 to 10. Then I have them stand up, put their hands over their head, smile and jump up and down for thirty seconds, all while shouting, "I love myself, I love the world!" Over and over. "I love myself, I love the world!"

After thirty seconds, they sit back down and again, on a scale of 1 to 10, rate how they're feeling. Without a doubt, if they were feeling like a 4 before, they feel like an 8 after those thirty seconds. It sounds silly, but it works. How you feel is entirely within your control, and this simple exercise shows you have the power to affect your state whenever you want, simply by using your body.

We all have physical patterns for our behaviors. We associate certain tonalities, movements, and stances with specific emotions. Cloé Madanes, a family therapist with decades of experience, has explained this further in her work. When someone comes to her and says they're feeling sad, she understands the person isn't actually sad. They're just doing sad. I want my clients to train their bodies to constantly do happy, not sad. It's really that simple.

Steve Jobs was famous for his thinking walks. He almost never held meetings with another person while sitting down in a room, but instead by walking side by side with them. He wasn't the only notable person to do this throughout history. Charles Darwin, Albert Einstein, Charles Dickens, Beethoven—they were all famous for their thinking walks. They all used walking as a way to enter a deep reflection state, which is a state where the outside world almost fades away. You can't see it or hear it. You're so deep in thought that it becomes the only place you're able to connect complex ideas in a way that's both simple and powerful.

Something as simple as taking a walk can help you better

control your own state. It's in your control. You're not a child anymore. How you feel is up to you.

LIE NO. 2: YOU'RE BORN WITH IT (OR NOT)

Some people are just born to be positive, and others are not. You've probably heard that at some point in your life, right? Well, guess what? It's total shenanigans.

Like all of the honest signals of status we're highlighting in this book, state control is a muscle. Think about it this way: why does LeBron James go to preseason training camp? He's a six-foot-eight, 250-pound physical specimen with the speed of a point guard and the jumping ability of a dunk champion. He's the best damn player in the world. Why should he even bother with training camp? Simple—if he's not practicing day in, day out, like he does during the season, he's going to be out of shape. The endurance needed to play professional basketball is a muscle, and it must be trained. That's why a player as naturally gifted as LeBron needs training camp.

People are born with inherent tendencies—a tendency toward introversion, or a tendency toward risk-seeking. But these are just tendencies, and tendencies don't equal destiny. No one is born unhappy. They're just out of practice. Everyone has to train their muscles to get better, whether they're a marathoner, a cyclist, or a basketball player. Shit, I'm a perfect example of this.

When I held my very first seminar years ago, it was just four guys in a tiny coworking space I rented in Santa Monica. It started at 9:00 a.m., and by 11:00 a.m., I was absolutely drained. My brain begged me to stop, and I felt physically tired. I remember thinking, "How the hell am I going to teach six more hours today and eight more hours tomorrow?" I made it work, because I'm a champion, but now I go twelve hours straight with no issues at my seminars and workshops. It's a muscle that I've trained over the years.

LIE NO. 3: EVERYTHING THAT MAKES YOU FEEL GOOD IS GOOD

This is something that's incredibly pervasive in our culture. People tell other people all the time, "Listen, if it feels good to you, you should do it." That's such a dangerous way of thinking. The truth is not all things that make you feel good are actually good for you.

There are two schools of thought to this—hedonic and eudaimonic. Hedonic, which comes from hedonism, is the idea that everything is random and we can't make sense of life, so we might as well enjoy all of the pleasures we can. Drugs, alcohol, sex—YOLO, right? You only live once, so live it up.

Eudaimonia, on the other hand, is where people derive a sense of good feeling and emotion from a deeper sense of purpose and meaning in their lives. This is someone who's doing great things not only for themselves, but also the people they care about. This ties back into high-status destiny, as a person with a eudaimonic approach dedicates their life to something they feel is truly making the world a better place.

We all know people that fall into one of these two categories, and they both generally appear happy. But is one better than the other? A recent study was conducted to look at the cellular level, and if you want to avoid illnesses and live forever, the results will stun you. The study found that people with eudaimonic lifestyles had favorable gene expression profiles. In plainer terms, it showed that eudaimonic lifestyles decreased inflammation and strengthened the immune system.

Hedonic people, on the other hand, had the exact opposite reaction. They had an adverse expression profile involving high inflammation with low antiviral and antibody gene expression. It's fascinating stuff, because everyone studied felt good in the moment. But on a deeper, cellular level, the person with a eudaimonic lifestyle is significantly healthier and, in all likelihood, will live longer.

REACTIVE VERSUS NONREACTIVE

Our lives are full of people, environments, and circumstances. It's crucial to remember that all of those things are *out* of our control. People react in one of two ways to these external factors—reactive and nonreactive.

A reactive response allows your state to be completely affected by other people, circumstances, or your environment. A nonreactive response is when your state is less and less affected by those outside factors. Being nonreactive, in the words of Robert Louis Stevenson, is when "you are free from the domination of outward conditions." What a perfect definition.

When you become nonreactive, you're able to be a more rational human being. People affected by other circumstances let their emotions get the better of them and stop thinking clearly. High-status people are *always* in control of their state.

One of my all-time favorite examples of nonreactive state control dates back to 1943. A lot of people don't know this about John F. Kennedy, but before he became a senator

FAST ACTION EXERCISE: HIGH-STATUS HABIT

A space shuttle uses two large rocket boosters to provide the fuel and thrust for liftoff during the first two minutes of launch. Those boosters constitute about 60 percent of the rocket's weight, as they carry 2.5 million pounds of fuel. During the next eight to ten minutes, the space shuttle's extra fuel tank burns through more than 540,000 of gallons of liquid fuel, providing enough speed and velocity to break the Earth's gravity and atmosphere and send the shuttle hurtling into space.

Approximately 90 percent of the fuel is used in the first few minutes. Once it's in the frictionless environment of outer space, the shuttle requires very little fuel for propulsion to maintain its course. Your habits are incredibly similar: starting a new habit requires the majority of your energy. Just being aware of this is going to help you create new habits. As I always tell my clients, first you form your habits, and then they form you.

Most habits take about thirty days to take hold, according to research, but that can be deceptive. Like anything, the more you practice it, the quicker you will pick it up. Your habits are no different. If you only practice a new habit once a day, then it will take longer than thirty days. If you practice multiple times per day, it could take less than thirty days.

On average, we use the thirty-day window as a typical barometer, and we break that up into three phases. Days 1 to 10 are the resisting-mediocrity phase, during which your old, mediocre habits are going to be pulling you down. You've got to put in the effort to resist them. Days 11 to 20 are the defying-the-old phase, in which you start to build momentum toward the new habit. It's still not easy yet, but it's easier than the first ten days. Days 21 to 30 are the adaptation phase, which is the point where you begin to float through space like the space shuttle. You still need to focus and avoid slipups, but once you get past day 30, it's going to become a habit for you.

Research also shows that reinforcement through awards at certain junctures along the habit-formation path during those thirty days can actually accelerate change and make it more permanent. Let's talk about how to do that:

STEP 1
What's something that would be a fun and healthy reward for you? I want you list ten options. It can be anything you enjoy doing: playing basketball, painting, taking a day trip with friends, eating a favorite dessert, getting a massage. Literally anything that you enjoy.

STEP 2

Create a reinforcement schedule for yourself before the start of the habit-formation process. On day 1, give yourself a reward. On day 3, the same. Continue to reward yourself on days 6, 10, 15, 21, and 28. Small rewards will ensure you stay on the successful habit-formation path.

STEP 3

Schedule a jackpot reward for day 35. Make this special reward three to five times bigger than the other ones. If you've been consistent for thirty-five straight days of self-correction and status practice, not only will you be the highest-status version of yourself that you've ever been, but you'll get to enjoy a massive jackpot bonus.

BONUS

This last step, called "taking away," isn't necessary for everyone, because it's a little hard core, but if you're feeling adventurous, give it a shot. On top of setting a jackpot reward for yourself at the end, you're going to set a consequence if you don't get there. Set something that can be taken away from you.

One of my personal favorites for this is donating $100 to a charity you wouldn't normally support. It's taking something away from you, but it's still helping others.

and eventually President of the United States, he was in the U.S. Navy. While at sea, his ship was sunk by a Japanese ship and he ended up stranded on an island with the rest of his crew. They had no water or food and were sitting ducks just waiting on an island. If the Japanese found them first, they would have ended up as POWs. Some of the remaining ten crew members lost their ability to control their state. They wanted to give up, but JFK wasn't like that. He stayed cool, calm, and collected. He stayed nonreactive.

JFK led the men to another small island a few miles' swim away, all while pulling an injured crewman despite

Kennedy's own back injury. Later on in life, one of his good friends said about JFK, "No set of circumstances can lick a boy like Jack." JFK himself later said he envisioned the experience as a story he could one day tell others to inspire them. How awesome is that? JFK never confused the page for the book. He believed that experience, no matter how dire it seemed, was only going to be a single page in the book of his life filled with dozens of chapters.

We can all learn from JFK. The story at the end of your life is going to be one hell of a book if you simply give yourself the gift of fighting through and overcoming major challenges. Think about it: no one wants to read a book about someone's life where they got up every day, went to the same job, came home, and went to bed. That's boring as fuck. It's the crazy, unexpected challenges and your ability to control your state while you fight through them that will make the story of your life that much more interesting.

HIGH-STATUS STATE CONTROL PRACTICES

There are six different practices that will help you master your state control: interpretation awareness, health and nutrition, physical anchoring, thought loops, physical challenges, and meditation. Let's tackle them, one-by-one:

Have you ever heard the story of the founding of the city of Alexandria in Egypt? No? Well, allow me enlighten you. Alexander the Great was well on his way to taking over the entire world when he arrived in Egypt in 332 BC. At that point, Egypt was like the center of the universe, and he wanted to build a big, booming, bustling city there—named after him, of course.

He sought an ideal area with access to the ocean for this city. After searching the surrounding areas, he finally found a perfect spot to build. He hadn't expected to find something so quickly, so all of the people in his retinue who were considered builders weren't exactly prepared with final blueprints. He didn't care. I mean, shit, he's Alexander the Great. He took action immediately, without hesitation. One of his soldiers recommended outlining the city with the excess grain they had in their stores. Great idea, right? Alexander thought so, too. They spent the rest of the day laying out grain in the shape of their future city.

The following morning, Alexander steps outside to look upon their work, and almost all of the grain is gone. It just vanished overnight. What happened? Well, they forgot there were things called birds that fly around in the sky and love to eat grain. Back then, *everyone* was superstitious, including Alexander. This was taken has a terrible omen.

Alexander asked his sages to interpret the meaning of the message. Their response might surprise you. Instead of feeding his fear and suggesting he abandon his plans for Alexandria, the sages said the city would be so successful and produce so much food that even the birds wouldn't go hungry. People would flock to it like birds, they said. Alexander, buoyed by this interpretation, saw the building of Alexandria to its end, and it stood as an epicenter of the world for hundreds of years.

This is an example of interpretation awareness. Things happen, but they don't mean anything to us. They don't have any effect on our emotional state or our mood until we decide what meaning we're going to give them. You're the one who has control over how you interpret a situation. You should always interpret things in a positive way, and there's an easy trick to doing so. Ask yourself a question: when something happens, remember that you don't have to accept the meaning that 99 percent of other people would derive from it. Instead, ask yourself, "I know this doesn't look good, but if I wanted this to mean something good, what could it mean?" Or, "How would someone like Alexander the Great or Oprah Winfrey interpret this?"

HEALTH AND NUTRITION

It's going to be really hard for someone who is tossing

down fast food and processed food all day long to maintain a good, positive, resourceful state all the time. Let's be honest: a Big Mac a day keeps the millions away.

Health and nutrition are important to your state control. These four practices will help you maintain a more positive state.

- **Sweat every day:** You don't have to do three hours of yoga or Pilates every day, nor do you have to look like a ripped Instagram model. It could be lifting weights, doing a workout at home, shooting some hoops, or running with your dog. Just do something that makes you break a real sweat every day.
- **Eat real food:** If it comes from a box or a bag, don't eat it. If it comes wrapped in paper, like a McDonald's cheeseburger, don't eat it. Stick to the real foods—fruits, vegetables, nuts, and meat.
- **Eat the rainbow:** This piggybacks on the last bullet point, but you want to make sure you're not just eating greens or red meats. Eat apples, mangoes, bananas, strawberries, raspberries. Different colors usually indicate different kinds of vitamins and minerals, so eat as many colors as possible.
- **Fast:** Fast either for twenty-four hours one day a week, or follow the daily 16:8 plan, which entails fasting for sixteen hours and consuming all of your

caloric intake during an eight-hour window. Fasting accelerates our fat-burning systems and is a great reset for our metabolism. This allows cellular cleansing to happen, which is crucial for our bodies to repair damaged cells. When you're constantly eating food, your body diverts energy from cellular cleansing to digestion. And when we give our body time for this cellular cleanse, the body can rid itself of damaged or malfunctioning parts of cells. This includes damaged mitochondria, which can lead to accelerated cellular damage and aging, as well as chronic diseases.

PHYSICAL ANCHORING

When I have the people at my seminars jump up and down while shouting, "I love my life, I love the world," I'm not doing it to make for good TV. I'm doing it because it's literally rewiring their brains for more happiness, more resourcefulness, and more passion. When they do that, good emotions are literally being created inside their bodies. By mixing this with speaking out loud, we create a physical anchor. Later on, when they're back home and want to feel good, they can just reenact the same move, and the positive emotions will erupt inside of them again. It's a remarkable tool for any high-status human being.

Any time you feel your state going down, or you're starting to feel fatigued, or something happens and it's affecting you, I want you to do something unique. Do something big and physical. Jumping up and down and screaming, "I love myself, I love the world," is a great option. Just do something that gets your entire body moving, and do it for between ten and thirty seconds. It's a reset for your state, and you'll notice it immediately.

THOUGHT LOOPS

We've highlighted some thought loops in previous chapters, and many of them apply now. With eye contact, for instance, I suggested the perspective reset thought loop of "Am I going to die?" Simply saying that to yourself in the moment can help alleviate any anxiety.

There are a million different thought loops at your disposal, but my favorite is also one of the simplest. Just tell yourself, "I love myself." Repeat it over and over a few times. It will do amazing things for your state.

You can come up with your own thought loops, too, as long as they are positive statements that are easy to repeat. It takes the focus off anything negative. Some other examples include "I love the world," "The world is great," and "I deserve the best the world has to offer." If you're preparing for a job interview, something like "I'm the best candidate by far and you know it" would work well.

Thought loops should be personal and unique to you, incorporating words and adjectives that vibe with the kind of person you are. Just make sure they are positive and easy to repeat.

PHYSICAL CHALLENGES

This practice involves putting yourself through things that are physically difficult, while keeping your body relaxed and calm. This recalls the cold shower exercise from earlier in this book. If you can calmly withstand cold water soaking your body for ten, twenty, thirty seconds, or longer, then there is nothing the world can throw at you that will get you off balance.

Other effective physical challenges include isometric deep lunges, which are standard lunges that you hold in place for as long as possible, and wall sits, the old middle school favorite where you hold a sitting motion with your back against a wall for as long as possible.

These exercises create tension in the body. That's why people shake, curse, or even scream if they hold these positions long enough. What state control does is raise threshold for the amount of tension you can withstand without needing to release it. High-status people not only handle tension but bask in it.

If you can hold a deep lunge or wall sit for two or three minutes, all while staying relaxed, you'll be able to access state control through physical challenges.

MEDITATION

Never go a day without meditation. It's that important. You don't have to sit cross-legged and repeat "om, om" over and over. You don't need to find a hidden cave in Asia. Not all meditation is a cliché. You can meditate using an app on your phone. You can take a long walk by yourself, which is a moving meditation. Prayer is another form of meditation.

The form doesn't matter as long as you're doing something every day to meditate. Start small, just for a few minutes each day. Again, this is a muscle you will have to train.

Meditation teaches you to remain calm and grounded in the middle of a storm. It also builds patience, which is important for high-status state control.

WHAT-IFS

These are some of the common questions I get about state control. Let's address them one by one:

WHAT IF I'M IN A TOUGH SPOT?

It happens to the best of us. You just find yourself stuck in a rut and nothing can get you out of it. It's important to remember that what you resist, persists. If you continue to tell yourself, "I can't get out of this funk," then you're essentially commanding your body to stay in the funk.

What you want to do is change that thought loop in your mind to something positive. Instead of saying, "I can't get out of this funk," simply say, "I haven't found the way out of this funk yet." Don't ignore the funk. Once you accept it, it will begin to dissipate.

WHAT IF I'M TOO SERIOUS?

Once you accept the funk you find yourself in, I want you to go to a mirror and look at yourself. Say out loud what's on your mind. "I feel awful right now." "I feel like shit right now." "I will never be successful." It doesn't matter what it is, just say what you're thinking out loud.

Repeat it over and over while getting progressively louder.

Make sure you include the words *right now*. It'll return perspective to your brain and emotions. Eventually you'll be screaming, "I will never be successful!" Guess what will happen? You'll start laughing. How can you not? It sounds absurd to shout "I will never be successful" over and over. Your concern will dissipate almost immediately.

HOW LONG WILL IT TAKE?

High-status state control is a muscle, and like any muscle, it has to be trained repeatedly. You wouldn't go to the gym once and expect to become ripped, right? But you will be surprised how quickly you can gain better control of your state through the practices we highlighted earlier.

I'd say about 90 percent of my clients tell me that within two weeks of practice, they wake up in a positive, excited mood. It might not be perfect twenty-four hours a day, and that's OK. It's a process. The more you work on it, the better it becomes.

You will be able to develop your state control faster than you could lose forty pounds of body weight or build up massive biceps, but here's the key: that change has to start now.

WHAT TO DO NEXT

We've covered what state control is, how crucial it is to your high-status future, and how the six practices will help you develop it. Before we move on to the next chapter on high-status carefreeness, there are three goals I want you to accomplish in the next week.

- **Set a health and nutrition schedule:** Are you eating in the best way possible for your state? If not, write out a plan for the next week that you can follow. Fast for twenty-four hours one day—or follow the 16:8 plan, if you prefer that—and eat the rainbow.
- **Begin physical anchoring:** Start slowly with this. In the next week, when you don't feel great, try one of the physical anchoring exercises we highlighted earlier. Since you're just starting out with this, I'd recommend doing it somewhere private. Try it two or three times a day and see it if works for you, as it has for more than one million people worldwide already.
- **Begin meditating:** If you've never meditated before, start out with three minutes per day for the next seven days. It can be sitting down, walking, or prayer, but just make sure it's three minutes.

If you begin with these three goals in the next week, you'll notice your state improving on a daily basis. As you continue to get more comfortable with all these practices, your state control will skyrocket.

When you're in a great state, it not only signals high status to others, but you'll find your decision-making becomes sharper, because you're so much more relaxed, positive, and resourceful. You'll be making decisions from a place of power and abundance, instead of fear and scarcity, like so many people do. You will also exude an aura of carefreeness, which is the seventh signal of high status. Carefreeness is an integral aspect of high status, one that almost no one teaches or talks about, and it's crucial to developing the magnetic, charismatic personality that attracts others naturally. You want that, don't you? Of course, you do. Let me show you how to get it.

Chapter Eight

HIGH-STATUS CAREFREENESS

———

Most of the people we meet in life can be divided into two different categories—carefree and worry-prone. There isn't usually much of an in-between area. The people we meet that are carefree seem to be breezing through life with a merry indifference. They're relaxed, they have good vibes, and they tend to just go with the flow of life. Worry-prone people are the exact opposite. It's almost as if carefree people have figured out a magic formula to life that worry-prone people haven't.

When we meet a carefree person who's giving off great vibes, we want to spend more time around them. They are naturally attractive in that regard. A common misconception about being high status is that you must be ultra-goal-oriented, with no down time to relax. That couldn't be farther from the truth. High-status people, whether they are goal-oriented or not, have a sense of carefreeness about them.

I've been starting most of these chapters off with a story, but I'm going to throw a curveball at you and open with an exercise. Don't worry, it's an easy one called the circles of concern and influence. Take a piece of paper and draw a big circle, then draw another smaller circle inside it.

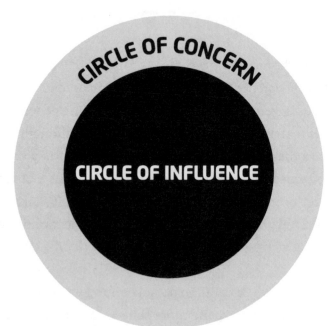

In the space between the two circles, I want you to write down everything that's on your mind. It doesn't matter if it's important or minor, happening tomorrow or five years from now. Just take three minutes to do a brain dump. After three minutes, go through everything you wrote down and put a star next to all the things that are directly within your control. For most people, about 40 to 50 percent of the things they listed will be within their control. What did your results look like?

Take all the things you starred and rewrite them inside the smaller inner circle. That is your circle of influence. When people who have mastered high-status carefreeness do this exercise, typically about 80 percent of their thoughts are directly within their control. If only about half of your thoughts are in your circle of influence right now, don't worry: that number will grow as you develop your high-status carefreeness.

But what about the thoughts on the paper you didn't star? Those are things taking up your mental energy, time, focus, attention, and concentration, but you will never be able to influence or change them. Those are the things you have absolutely no control over. They form the circle of concern.

Carefree people do not have *zero* concerns. That's a misconception. They just have a much bigger circle of influence than circle of concern. People who are carefree are keenly aware and highly focused on the things they can control. This makes sense, right? So much stress and anxiety in our lives comes from shit that is completely out of our control.

THE POWER OF CAREFREENESS

OK, *now* it's story time, and it's going to be another Steve Jobs tale. If you couldn't already tell, Jobs was pretty damn high status. Jobs was at a dinner party in 1987 with King Juan Carlos I of Spain. Ross Perot—yup, the same businessman who twice ran for President in the 1990s—was a key investor in Jobs' company NeXT, so he introduced him to the Spanish king. Not long after being introduced, Jobs and Juan Carlos disappeared for like twenty minutes. Perot looked for them but couldn't find them.

Eventually, he spotted them together at the center of the main dining table, carrying on a relaxed, jovial conversation. After it ended, he asked Jobs what the two had just talked about. "I have no idea," he said, "but I just sold him a computer!" They both started cracking up. "You sold the king of Spain a computer?" Perot repeated. "Yeah, he doesn't have one. Can you believe it?" Jobs replied.

Steve Jobs was not intimidated by royalty. He was carefree. High-status people are excited about where they're going and what they're doing in life, so their focus stays on their behavior, not the outcome of a situation. Jobs wasn't worried about impressing the king. He was focused on having a great conversation, practicing his sales skills, and enjoying the fun of just going for it. If the king had said no, or ended their conversation early, Jobs wasn't going to judge himself by that outcome. Being carefree means you don't focus on the outcome, but rather on your own actions. Our own actions are entirely within our circle of influence, while most outcomes are within our circle of concern.

Legendary college basketball coach John Wooden believed that success was peace of mind resulting from self-satisfaction and knowing you put forth your best effort. It's a bit of a tongue twister, but basically he believed success was measured by the effort and focus of his players in games, not the final score. That's a powerful—and rare—way of thinking. Most people fall prey to something called evaluation bias, which is the tendency to allow others' evaluations to hold more weight than your own. It doesn't matter whether those evaluations are good or bad, right or wrong, positive or negative. If you continuously rely on others' assessments, you become dependent on them. That always leads to negative consequences.

How many celebrities have we seen over the years that were driven to harmful behavior because of the constant evaluations from fans and critics? Heath Ledger, Marilyn Monroe, Whitney Houston, Billy Mays, Amy Winehouse— the list just goes on and on. These were all people who appeared successful on the outside but struggled internally, because they placed more stock in other people's evaluations than their own.

BE YOUR OWN COACH

External recognition tastes good in the mouth but bitter in the belly. What I mean by that is, receiving a positive evaluation will feel good in the moment, but as more time passes, it will feel bitter as you constantly put yourself under stress to replicate that feeling.

The cure to this is simple: start drinking from your own sources. What truly makes a person centered is the ability to absorb and rely on evaluations not from others, but from themselves. When you constantly absorb evaluations from the outside world, your path is no longer your own. It becomes everyone else's path.

If you find yourself relying on the evaluations of other people in your life, you *must* start listening to the coach who knows you best. That coach is you. You're going to evaluate yourself wholly on your own behaviors, not outcomes. That will allow you to center your life and give you peace of mind.

To use another sports metaphor, when playing tennis, you're taught to hold the racket handle with a light grip. If you squeeze it too hard, you'll develop a blister and, trust me, that shit hurts. I was recently at the Camelback Resort in Scottsdale, Arizona, and decided to take a tennis lesson. I hadn't played in years, so I forgot how to hold the racket. I had a blister the size of a jelly bean for the next three days. You've got to live life with a light grip. Once you do that, you'll become more carefree, and when you become carefree, you'll be more naturally alluring to others. You'll enjoy life and live each day moment to moment. You'll have the freedom to be playful, to express yourself fully, to negotiate better, to meet more people, to hear the word *yes* more often, and to achieve your goals faster and with more enjoyment. Honestly, what the fuck could be better than that?

BEING PURSUED VERSUS BEING A PURSUER

There is power that comes from being the one who is pursued by others, as opposed to being the one who pursues. Human beings are hardwired to pursue that which retreats from us. Knowing that, it makes sense that high-status people are the ones being pursued by others, and not the other way around.

There is a fine line here though. It has to be natural. You can't retreat on purpose to get the result of someone pursuing you, because that's not carefree. That's becoming dependent on an outcome that is out of your control. In that scenario, you've stopped judging yourself on your own behavior and started grading yourself based on outcomes. That is *not* the way of a high-status, carefree person.

Carefree people appear to retreat naturally for two reasons. First, they don't need anyone else's approval, and second, their high-status destiny keeps them constantly in motion, on their path. They are not retreating from others on purpose, but instead are continuously moving forward on their path.

Trust me, you will stand out even more in this digital, social media-obsessed world we live in today. With cell phones and Instagram and Facebook and all that other shit, people have literally trained themselves to be approval rats, just constantly chasing the next online like or comment. People will even post something online and, if they aren't pleased with the amount of likes or comments it gets within that first hour, they'll delete it. All they're doing is training themselves to be completely reliant on other people to feel good. Since this is now, sadly, becoming the norm, if you become one of the rare few who are truly carefree, you're going to have all the approval rats chasing you. Whether you want that to happen or not... well, that's up to you. But it's *going* to happen because carefree people are pursued by others.

THE KING OF COOL

Just like Steve Jobs, I have a deep, deep appreciation and admiration for Dean Martin. He is just an amazing example of someone who was carefree and seemed to breeze along through life. I mean, come on, the guy was known as the "King of Cool." If that doesn't scream carefree, what does? Frank Sinatra was the most famous member of the Rat Pack, but the women loved—and pursued—Dean Martin more than anyone.

One thing Martin loved even more than the ladies was playing golf. While all the other Rat Packers would stay out until 4:00 a.m. partying, Martin would make sure he was in bed by midnight so he could get up for his morning tee times. One time he was out at a course in Las Vegas and he heard a kid from the UCLA golf team was also there. One thing led to another, and Martin agreed to play against the kid for $20,000. That was a lot of money back then. Shit, it's still a lot of money. They ended up playing and the kid just destroyed Martin. Seriously, he beat him on every hole and won all $20,000.

At the end of the round, the kid started apologizing. Martin, exhibiting the essence of carefreeness, simply replied, "Don't worry about it, kid. Remember, I can make it back faster than you can win it." Without question, that kid walked away thinking Dean Martin was one of the coolest people walking the planet.

Still not convinced Dean Martin is the epitome of carefreeness? I've got another quick story about the King of Cool that should change your mind. By the late 1960s, *The Dean Martin Show* was one of the most popular TV shows in America, but Martin was getting tired of the monotony involved with a weekly variety show. One night at dinner, he told his wife, "I'm just going to ask them for something crazy, like $30 million. That'll put a stop to this."

Martin met with the TV execs the following weekend, but instead of them canceling the show, Martin walked out with more money. A *lot* more money. I don't know how much he actually asked for, but I know he walked into the meeting making $40,000 an episode and walked out making $285,000 an episode. If Martin hadn't been carefree, the mere idea of asking for $30 million would have never even come to him. The ability to go into a negotiations meeting and ask for an astronomical salary increase in a relaxed manner requires a well-trained carefreeness muscle. The TV execs clearly recognized that and pursued Martin.

MYSELF AS AN EXAMPLE

At the time of writing this book, I'm in negotiations with an English celebrity to join his team as a consultant. I can't say the guy's name because nothing is finalized, but as of early 2017, he had 33 million followers on the major social media networks. For perspective, Oprah Winfrey had about 25 million followers. I know a number of the other guys that have already signed on to join this celebrity's team, and they're all pumped. But for me, it's not quite as black and white.

Being carefree allows you to recognize many different options. As a high-status individual, I'm simply keeping my options open. To me, it's not just a simple yes or no. For instance, maybe I don't sign a contract, but instead get a piece of the company itself. That's just one possible alternative.

It's been an ongoing process, but I'm the last one of their targets that's yet to sign anything. Because of that, they're coming back with more and more counteroffers, as they push harder and harder to get me on board. The most recent offers I've gotten have been greater than the offers of the people I know who've already signed with them. By the time this book is printed, I may have ultimately decided against joining this celebrity's team at all. I live a carefree life.

You know who also lives a carefree life? My man Harvey Specter on the TV show *Suits*. Even if you don't watch the show, here's all you need to know: Specter is a goal-oriented, successful, high-status character, but he's also very carefree. He'll be saving a billion-dollar company in court while cracking jokes at the same time.

There's one scene in particular that captures Specter's carefreeness. He's mentoring Mike, another one of the attorneys at the firm, and getting frustrated with him because Mike has given up on a problem. He says they have no options, which sets Specter off. Specter asks Mike what he'd do if someone put a gun to his head. Mike replies, "What are you talking about? You do what they say, or they shoot you." "Wrong," Specter shoots back. "You take the gun, or you pull out a bigger one, or you call their bluff, or you do any one of 146 other things." It's a great fucking scene, but to my point, Specter is carefree, so he can envision all these different options.

ALLURING VERSUS REPULSIVE

Think about the last person you met who had a repulsive personality. I'm not talking about their physical appearance, just their personality. I bet their personality gave off a sense that wanted something from their interaction with you. Whether they wanted you to see them as a tough guy, or as the boss, or they just wanted your attention. A repulsive personality is defined by a sense of neediness—a need for validation, a need for approval, a need to be liked. Neediness drives us away.

No one wants to come across as needy. We want to be alluring, which is equal parts attention and mystery. There's a hint of mystery about an alluring person because they're not overcommunicating. They're not broadcasting every single detail of their life on social media. They don't feel a need to do that to gain validation, because they are certain of themselves. Their circles of influence are big, and their circles of concern are small. We are drawn to people like this.

Overcommunicating makes you look like you're trying too hard, and people that try too hard aren't cool. People who are relaxed and nonchalant about life, on the other hand, typically are pretty damn cool. There's a great quote that's stuck with me for a long time on this subject: love never dies of starvation, but often of indigestion. If you're calling, texting, or communicating with someone too often, you're going to push them away. Overcommunication is the indigestion in this metaphor. Like too much food is bad for the stomach, too much neediness is bad for attraction. It's important sometimes to just let the other person wonder about you.

Before Dwight D. Eisenhower was President of the United States, he spent five years as the president of Columbia University. At one point during his tenure, a number of professors banded together to complain about students walking across the lawn on campus instead of the sidewalks. The lawn was the quickest, most direct path between buildings, while the sidewalks were more roundabout. When alerted to this, Eisenhower calmly told the professors, "Did you ever notice how much quicker it is to head directly where you're going? Why don't we just find out which route the students are going to take and just build the walks there?"

That's an alluring, carefree response, and it highlights the two sides of this coin. On one side, there was the reactive, needy behavior by the professors in blowing something as unimportant as where students were walking out of proportion. They were confined to a fixed set of rules. On the other side, there was a powerful, carefree response from Eisenhower, who knew the students were just going to take the most direct path no matter what. Like water, they went with the flow and adapted to the reality of the situation.

ADVENTUROUS VERSUS GRAVELIKE

I know a guy who makes $80,000 a month on the Internet. That's not his yearly income—that's what he's pulling in each and every month. Needless to say he's doing just *fine* financially. Yet this same guy won't leave his current full-time office as a programmer. His *annual* salary for that position? $60,000. Let's see—$80,000 per month versus $60,000 per year. Which would you choose?

He's genuinely afraid that the Internet will eventually collapse, or that a tech bubble will burst, or that his online business just won't last forever. This is someone who has trained himself to be as worry-prone as humanly possible. He is already living a gravelike existence. Choosing not to live adventurously is simply choosing not to live. Only a dead body is truly protected. Everything that lives is always in danger. Simply being alive is a hazard. As humans, we forget this. We think because we've built houses and other buildings that make us feel safe that we're protected, but the reality is that we're always in danger.

Friedrich Nietzsche always kept a personal motto

hanging on his wall. It read, "Live dangerously." Whenever anyone asked him why he wanted that displayed, he said, "Because my fear is tremendous and I never want to forget the truth." If you look at some people in today's world, they're basically dead already. It's sad but true. They settle into this pattern of convenience and monotony, and it's essentially a gravelike existence.

I once heard a story about a father and his young daughter, whom he had brought to a birthday party for one of her friends from school. The daughter was mesmerized by the sparkling birthday candles on the cake, the colorful balloons, and the lively singing of "Happy Birthday." She turned to her father and asked, "Daddy, were there such beautiful days when you were alive?" When children are young, they often see their parents as robots programmed to do the same things every day, instead of living people capable of enjoying the moment.

I've tried to be mindful of this in my own life and never allow gravelike monotony to take hold, but it wasn't until 2012 that I took my most adventurous leap of faith. I remember the moment vividly. I was at my usual gym, the Equinox Fitness Club in Santa Monica, doing rep after rep of bicep curls. I had been going to the gym almost every day for the previous few months, and I was definitely seeing the physical results. But as I looked around the gym as the same fucking people doing the same fucking exercises, it hit me: I was one of them. I was settling in a predictable routine, doing the same thing over and over every day. When that realization hit me, I dropped the weight in the middle of the set, left the gym, walked the four blocks back to my apartment, and booked a one-way ticket to Medellín, Colombia. I shit you not.

I don't know where the rush for Colombia came from. I hadn't been reading about Pablo Escobar, or watching a show about the country. I can't explain why I picked Colombia, but I knew I had to shake things up. I had to do something adventurous, and I had to do it at that exact moment. And, of course, what happened next? I told my roommate what I was doing, and he asked to join. An hour after that, another friend got on board. Later that week, two more friends joined in. We ended up spending three months in a beautiful penthouse on the top of a hill in Colombia.

Adventurous living is contagious. Human beings are made to move around. We were *not* meant to settle down in one place and stay there forever. Even if you own a house, you don't have to remain there every single day. The simple act of traveling can dramatically increase your carefree muscle.

In 2016, I visited Rome, Venice, Italy, Thailand, Amsterdam, London, Scotland, China, Hong Kong, and more. At this point in my life, I'm on a plane nearly 100 days a year. I don't say this to impress anyone. I force myself to travel, especially when I'm feeling comfortable, because it helps keep my carefree muscle active and strong. I understand it might not be feasible for you to travel as often as I have, but trust me, you have it in you. Even short weekend trips or day trips can make a difference. Embrace your inner humanity by getting up and moving around once in a while.

BUILDING YOUR CAREFREENESS

Carefreeness is in us all. Some people are just more out of practice than others. In that sense, it's no different than a muscle on your body. You've got to work out to get stronger, and you've got to practice different techniques to strengthen your carefreeness.

VERBALS

Start by practicing carefreeness in your conversations. One of my favorite things to have clients do is practice this when extending invitations. For instance, most guys, when they ask a girl out, will say something like, "Hey, I'm free Friday night. Let's go grab a drink and a movie," or, "Let's grab a drink and dinner."

This is basically the standard line for date invitations, and it's simply not effective anymore. Why? Because it immediately puts pressure on the girl—a pressure to say yes—and no one likes feeling pressured. One-on-one dates are stressful—what to wear, what to talk about, what happens at the end of the night. If you simply attach a rider to every invitation, it changes the whole dynamic, and it highlights your magnetic carefreeness. So instead of saying, "Hey, I'm free Friday night, let's grab drinks," first ask, "Hey, when are you free this weekend—Friday or Saturday?" After she tells you Friday is better, for example, follow up with, "Cool. Let's grab drinks Friday, if you think you can hang at this level." Something as simple as "if you think you can hang at this level" immediately lightens the mood, removes the pressure, and establishes you as that carefree person.

Another verbal exercise is simply ending a phone call first. It's amazing how long some people drag on phone conversations. Don't be one of them. When you're done, you're done. Hang up the damn phone.

Your everyday errands offer another perfect opportunity to practice verbal carefreeness. Whether you're checking out at a grocery store, paying for a burrito at Chipotle, or otherwise out in public somewhere, don't be afraid to crack a simple, self-entertaining joke with people. More than likely, you're only going to deal with these people for thirty seconds, so use it as an opportunity to train the muscle. Make a joke that's funny to you, but don't worry about whether the other person finds it funny. Remember, that's an outcome, and you can't control it. For example, I was recently at the grocery store, and the girl at the register asked for my phone number to see if I was in the store's system. My response? "You're not going to start blowing up my phone, are you?" We both shared a laugh. She may or may not have asked for my phone number in return. Simple. Carefree.

Pick one of these verbal techniques and start practicing it now. Don't put it off. Practice it today and tomorrow. Notice how other people respond to you.

BODY LANGUAGE

You're going to start with something I call the foot trick. We're taught from a young age how to lie with our faces, but we're never taught how to lie or deceive with our feet. In fact, a lot of times you'll find feet are the most honest signal of how someone is feeling.

Take note of this in your future conversations. If you're talking to someone and one of their feet starts pointing off to the left or right instead of directly at you, something else is on their mind. It's not that they dislike you. They might have a meeting to get to, or an appointment, or something else on their schedule. When I notice this, I'll say, "You have somewhere to be, don't you?" They'll look at you with a thankful expression as they think, "How did you read my mind?"

Be aware of this when you have conversations with people. On the flip side, put yourself in the feet—literally—of the other person in this example. By pointing one of your feet out and casually bouncing up and down on your toes, you're conveying to the other person you're more carefree about the conversation. It's not do-or-die for you.

Practice this, along with the verbal technique you selected, today and tomorrow. Again, observe how other people react to you.

Another body language trick is an old favorite: when in doubt, lean out. People who are worry-prone are always leaning in. Don't fall prey to that. People who are carefree are laid back and relaxed. When in doubt, lean out.

MEDITATION

Here's another one we've covered at length, but it bears repeating. Meditation is so important not only for your state control, but for your carefreeness. It allows many of the attachments that people have to dissipate. A calmer, more focused mind is a carefree mind.

Meditation is something everyone, everywhere can do, regardless of previous experience. Start small—just three minutes at first, like we highlighted in the last chapter, is perfect—and steadily increase the length of your meditations.

DESTINY KEEPS YOU ON TRACK

The most important thing to understand about your internal carefreeness is that it's fueled by your high-status destiny. Whatever your vision is in life, it's so valuable to you and takes up so much of your time, attention, and focus that you naturally start to assign less significance to everything else. Twitter likes, Instagram comments, text messages—all of that bullshit starts to mean less and less. Your high-status destiny will push you far beyond those types of insignificant distractions.

Something else to keep in mind: every plane is off course for 99 percent of every flight. Bet you didn't know. This is something known as course-tracking, and it basically means that even though the plane is never perfect, it's still on its path to its destination. When Steve Jobs sat down with the king of Spain, he wasn't worried about whether he was on course 100 percent of the time. He was focused on his behaviors and striving to make himself better. He was always course-correcting toward his high-status destiny.

WHAT-IFS

There are two common questions I typically get asked about high-status carefreeness. The first one is, "Is carefreeness just not caring?" The truth is...sometimes. Remember, it's easier to your act your way into a new way of thinking than it is to think your way into a new way of acting. Keeping that in mind, you're going to be practicing all these techniques until they become natural. Model yourself after someone you perceive as carefree. Eventually, you'll start receiving similar responses from others, and it will give you a different feeling than you've been used to. There will certain situations in your life where you simply don't care, and that's great—that means you're becoming carefree.

The other question I hear all the time is, "Jason, is this going to make me an asshole?" Absolutely not. People love putting labels on shit, and they especially love labeling your change in a negative way because your upward movement frightens them. I have a friend who recently left his nine-to-five job, which he hated, to pursue a career in copywriting. He loves writing and selling, so it's a perfect fit. His family, however, has only hounded him, claiming he's put his entire future in jeopardy. They're constantly begging him to "return to his senses." Of course, when they say "his senses," they mean "their wishes." Why do people who love us do that? It's a weapon to keep you from changing. Change can be intimidating for other people and difficult for them to accept, but don't let that deter you. Remember, you're on your path to your high-status destiny, and the hard truth is they probably aren't.

Stay on your path, focus on the different techniques highlighted in this chapter, and you'll become truly carefree, which is the most attractive high-status trait. And honestly, what a perfect segue, because I just hit you with some high-status truth, which is what the next chapter is all about. In a world full of wussies and self-deceivers, you'll stand out by expressing your true feelings while maintaining your power and strength. I'll show you how, right now.

Chapter Nine

HIGH-STATUS TRUTH

———

How would you define the word *truth*? Webster's Dictionary has a great definition: "that which is." I love it. It's so succinct, yet so correct. In fact, if you really want to have some fun, the next time you're having a few drinks with friends, ask them to define the word *truth*. You'll get a lot of confused looks, followed by some great discourse as they begin to realize they've never truly considered something so important to the happiness and success of their lives.

It's hard to define truth. To me, it's aiming to get as close to objectivity as possible. That looks good written on paper, but here's the problem: everyone's brain is caked in bullshit. This isn't meant as a dig at any of you, my loyal readers. It's just a reflection of the world we live in.

With the way the news media works in conjunction with social media, there's often a serious difference between that which is and that which is reported. Everyone's interpretation of what happened in a given news story is going to be different. We're flooded with endless points of view, analyzing and dissecting things over and over to the point of nausea. Their storytelling ends up replacing reality with their version of reality. The truth is rarely seen and rarely heard in the world we live in now.

A woman asked me an interesting question at one of my recent events. She had a close friend who had poured most of her life savings into creating an app, but she felt strongly the app was doomed to fail. "I don't want to tell her because I don't want to hurt her feelings. What do you think I should do?" Most people avoid saying what they think to save a relationship, friendship, or connection. The reality is when you hold back, you're actually pushing the person farther away from the true you. Even worse, you're clipping their wings at the same time by allowing them to continue with something that won't benefit them. That girl's friend could have been doing something better with her time and energy, but she hadn't gotten a single memo from the world, because no one spoke up to her. My answer to her question was simple: unless you're an asshole and want your friend to continue struggling, yes, tell her.

I know you're reading this right now and thinking of the specific situations in your own life and relationships with others, whether it's not sharing how you truly feel about their behavior, or how you feel about the way they dress, talk, or communicate. Maybe there's a boundary in your current relationship with a significant other, friend, or even family member that's making you unhappy, but because it seems difficult or painful to give truth, you instead continue to avoid the issue. Yet the truth is, the more you avoid it, the bigger the problem gets, and the further you distance yourself from them.

A few years ago, I said, enough. I had grown so tired of everyone just avoiding these issues. It seemed like all my conversations were packed with bullshit. Everyone was dancing around the real issues. I wanted to see what would happen if I just started telling the truth. Admittedly, in the beginning, I started off too extreme, but I had to find the right balance.

One of the first times I tried this, I was sitting with my buddies, as one of them talked about a girl he liked who hadn't texted him back. The other guys were like, "OK, man, break it down for us. What happened?" He then went on a ten-minute spiel about their first date, what they did, what they talked about—on and on and on. Everyone in the room knew the same thing I did: this girl just wasn't into him. But no one said a goddamn thing. I stepped up to the plate. "Dude, I love you, and that's why I'm telling you this right now. She's not interested in you. She obviously doesn't have good taste, but that's OK. We'll go out tonight and find someone better." There's a short period, maybe ten minutes, of painful acceptance. It sucks to hear something like that, but he was so grateful that someone actually gave it to him straight.

High-status truth became a way of life for me years ago, and it still is today. Now the hundreds of thousands of people I've taught to give truth lead happier, more joyful, more fulfilled lives and have happier, more joyful, more fulfilled relationships with people. Their relationships are based in the context of truth and honesty, as opposed to verbal constipation and bullshit. Which one would you rather have?

TRUTH IS PERSONAL

Not long before I started writing this book, I came to the inescapable realization that I was personally unhappy with my own life. I just wasn't excited about life. In most people's eyes, I should have been: I'm a self-made millionaire with a mission I'm superpassionate about, a beautiful girlfriend, a gorgeous house, and connections with celebrities and other high-status people all over the world. How could Jason Capital be unhappy with his life?

The more I analyzed everything and was honest with myself, I came to understand I wasn't happy with the way my relationship was set up. See, in relationships, sometimes you want closeness and other times you want aloneness. People usually have an innate tendency toward one or the other. Maybe you feel better when you're close to your partner, or maybe you feel suffocated if you're too close all the time. When an aloneness person feels too much closeness, they begin to feel unsafe in the relationship. When a closeness person feels too much distance, they too begin to feel unsafe in the relationship.

In all relationships, safety is the most important thing. And yet in my own relationship, I—the big dating coach—had allowed things to get unsafe. My girlfriend is very independent, but she leans toward the closeness side of the spectrum. I am the opposite. I lean toward the aloneness side. I'd set up my life so there wasn't enough aloneness, or "me time," and it was making me feel unhappy. How do you let someone know that you love them with every fiber of your being, yet need more time alone without them feeling hurt or taking it personally? This is why becoming a strong, open, honest, high-status communicator is incredibly important. I communicated honestly and openly with her about this, in the same ways I'm going to show you in this chapter, and since then, our relationship and partnership have never been stronger.

Truth is not always easy, believe me. Shit, it was hard for me just to share that story about my girlfriend and me with hundreds of thousands of people I've never met, but it conveys such an important point: telling the truth is difficult. Having those types of conversations can cause tension or anxiety, and that's totally normal. What makes someone high status is the ability to stay the course, regardless of any feelings of anxiety or tension that might arise. The conversation between my girlfriend and me was *not* easy, but it needed to happen. Being able to communicate open and honestly with someone, while still being able to strengthen the bond between the two of you, is so powerful. Once you master this skill, you'll no longer have to worry about things like "I left that thing unsaid," or "I don't know how to have this conversation." There are specific ways to have these high-stakes, difficult conversations in a way that makes them easy and helpful for both parties.

THE POWER OF HIGH-STATUS TRUTH

While most people focus on the anxiety or tension that giving truth can create, they fail to consider the benefits, and there are several. The first benefit is obvious: you will stand out. We've already established that most people dance around the real issues with their friends, family, and significant others. By simply giving truth, you will refreshingly rare and authentic.

Beyond simply standing out, you will become better understood. People have an ingrained desire to feel understood. Ralph Nichols, who conducted the study of listening, said, "The most basic of all human needs is the need to understand and be understood." This makes sense, right? No one wants to walk away constantly having others misinterpret their feelings. Think about the friends you're closest with, the ones who you feel understand you on a deeper level. If you become someone who constantly exhibits high-status truth, it will become more obvious when something is bothering you.

I'll give you a quick example of this. I always tell people when I enter a business relationship with them that when I'm uncomfortable with something, my tendency is sit silently, pretending like I'm thinking about something, but, in reality, I'm just thinking about whatever has made me uncomfortable. I talk a lot, so it's pretty noticeable when I go quiet.

People who don't give truth would never share those kinds of personal traits, which can be really helpful in both business and personal relationships. I have one business partner in particular who, knowing how I handle uncomfortable situations, called me on it. We were in a follow-up meeting to review some of his tweaks for an idea we had worked on a few months earlier, and I didn't like the tweaks. We sat there for a minute before he said, "Jason, what's the friction that you're feeling inside right now?" What a genius fucking question. It snapped me right out of it and we resolved the entire issue.

Those who give high-status truth also exude a certain magnetism others don't. There's a certain signal their energy sends out. They're present, they're listening, they're hearing the real you, and they have no problem calling you on your bullshit.

John F. Kennedy is a shining example of someone who exuded magnetism through his ability to truly listen and give truth. When he was at Stanford University for graduate business classes, he was already well known. His parents were famous, of course, and some of the local newspapers in Northern California had written about him. While he was eating lunch one day, Kennedy was approached by another student, Henry James. The two struck up a conversation and Kennedy invited him to eat with him. Kennedy asked James question after question: Where are you from? Where did you graduate from? What did you study? How did you do there? What are you doing here? Within five minutes, Kennedy knew James's life story. Kennedy had a focus on learning and connecting, not impressing anyone. If he wasn't someone who gave truth and spoke freely, he wouldn't have peppered his new friend with questions. But that's what Kennedy did with everyone he met, because he genuinely wanted to connect and learn about people. Billionaire Charlie Munger has said curiosity is one of the greatest tools at our disposal, and you can't be curious without being able to give truth freely.

High-status truth will also help others open up. Bill Gates was notorious for his confrontational style of communication—more on that later. But he was also known for going first. When you want someone to do something—in this case, give truth—you've got to first do it yourself. His coming into meetings totally extreme and bombastic, saying things like, "That's the stupidest fucking idea I've ever heard," creates an environment where everyone can be totally honest with each other and not take it personally. And yes, Gates really did say things like that to the people he worked with. You certainly don't have to go that far. Personally, I'm not a fan of the word *stupid*. Why? I don't know, it's just...stupid. See, there it goes again! Anyway. Onward.

YOUR APPROACH

There's a right way and wrong way to approach high-status truth. Let's break down a few different dos and don'ts.

- **Do make the person feel safe.** Make sure the person you're sharing truth with knows you're coming from a caring perspective. Come into the situation with genuine, good intentions for yourself, them, and your relationship. It has to take place in a context of safety, and there's no faking that. You have to truly care, without judgment or expectation.
- **Don't make them feel threatened.** This should be obvious after that last bullet point, but it's important to keep in mind. If someone punches you in the face, what do you do? You either fight back or run away—fight or flight. Well, a threatening statement of truth will cause the same reaction.
- **Do help them.** What about criticizing people? Is that giving truth? You certainly don't want to say, "Hey, you suck at making coffee." That's threatening. Instead, point out to them what great coffee tastes like and let them connect the dots. That's what a high-status communicator does.
- **Don't overcommunicate.** Every single thought that crosses your mind doesn't need to be verbalized. This is the problem with Facebook, Twitter, and Instagram, right? People tweet or post in the heat of

the moment, without thinking. If you're constantly just spewing everything on your mind all the time, the truth you give loses all its oomph and value. Keep your powder dry. Use it in key moments and situations in your life.

TRAINING YOUR TRUTH

Truth, like all of the other signals of high status we've covered so far, is a muscle. It will take a little practice, but with time, you can master it. These exercises will help you get there.

AURELIUS EXERCISE

This one is named after the great Roman emperor Marcus Aurelius, and it's actually something he was known to do quite frequently. He would look at things that, in his opinion, people valued too highly, and he would define them more literally. Remember, truth is that which is. So, something like vintage wine? He would call that old grapes. Roasted meat? That was dead animal. He tried to get as close to reality as he could without painting these items in hyperbolic colors.

In our modern-day world, a viral celebrity post would be a sad person seeking attention. A Lamborghini? Just a metal container for transportation. Not only is this exercise fun to do, you can it anytime, anywhere.

RENAMING TRAINING CEREMONY

This is a rite of passage for everyone who becomes high status. Like the Aurelius exercise, this one can be fun, but you've got to actually interact with other people. After you finish reading this chapter, you're going to try this on the next five people you meet. It has to be people—and names—you don't already know. You're going to rename them.

If they say, "Hey, it's great to meet you, I'm Mark," you're going to reply, "You know, it's funny. You don't really look like a Mark. You look more like a Steve." What you're doing with this exercise isn't abusive, mean, or hurtful. It's just practice in communicating in unfamiliar but more powerful ways. You're going to practice saying something most people would be uncomfortable saying, and that's the whole point.

The second part of this ceremony is similar, but with a fun tweak. You're going to do the renaming bit again with the next five people you meet, but you're going to do it while modeling a high-status character. Pick someone from a movie, TV show, or any other medium, whom you recognize as a truth-giver that just calls shit like it is. Model their tonality and nonchalance when you're renaming the next five people.

You'll notice a totally different response than the first time through. Don't worry—it's all part of the development. You'll be amazed how quickly you begin to internalize how to give truth, and with what tonality to give it.

SOMETHING LEFT UNSAID

Think of one conversation you've been avoiding for way too long. From the thousands of people I've met from over 150 countries in my life, I have yet to meet a single person who wasn't keenly aware of at least one conversation they've been avoiding.

Identify one conversation you've been avoiding and answer the following questions:

- What has avoiding this conversation cost me so far?
- If I never have this conversation, what will it cost me?
- If I do have this conversation, what is the likely outcome?
- When will I have this conversation?

Answer all these questions honestly. This is going to be challenging, but it's so important. List out all the different answers that come to mind and analyze them. If you can see, on paper, what this delayed conversation has cost you already or will cost you in the future, compared to the most likely outcome, it's not going to seem as bad as you think.

If you then approach the person and let them know you have the best intentions in mind for everyone involved, I guarantee it's going to bring you much closer to that person than continuing to push them away. The final step, of course, is to set a date and time to have the conversation. You *can* do this. It seems daunting at first, but take it slow and you'll get there.

MENTAL COMMITMENT TRICK

Remember, it's going to be a process. A lot of times people will start giving high-status truth, but they will let their state affect it. It's easy to give truth when you're in a great state, right? But what about when you're in a lousy state? When that happens, it's easier to let things pass by or come up with an excuse. Shit, I still go through this. No one is perfect.

I recommend typing this out in your phone so you have access to it at all times. Save a note somewhere that reads,

"The next time I get the opportunity to _____, I'm going to _____," and fill in the blanks. This will help set your brain to be aware of the specific thing you wanted to do but didn't do the previous time. It's a commitment and promise to yourself that you'll take that action. Years ago I met this girl on the Santa Monica Promenade. We hit it off, but when I had to go, instead of exchanging phone numbers with her, I let the fear of rejection win. I remember walking away, frustrated with myself for not taking action. But instead of lamenting the missed opportunity, I took a proactive and productive next step.

I whipped out my phone and opened a new note. I then typed, "Jason, the next time you meet someone and hit it off with them, will you ask for their number?" I read the question back to myself, thought about it for a second, then typed my response: *yes*.

You might think, "Well, if I write it in my phone today and forget about it for two weeks, what's the point?" Trust me, you'll be amazed at how quickly it pops back into your brain the next time around.

A QUICK PARABLE

As you become a high-status communicator, you'll understand how to share difficult things with people, but in a way that actually builds them up and strengthens the bond between you both. Stories, anecdotes, and parables are one of the absolute best ways to do this, and a favorite technique of the world's best communicators. I discovered the power of parables when I spoke to one of my friends recently.

My friend was stuck in a negative relationship. Everyone could tell he was being controlled and manipulated in a hurtful way by his girlfriend. He had stopped seeing his friends and family as much, and he was making decisions that didn't align with what he wanted to do in life. I knew it wasn't going to be easy to say, point blank, "Dude, I don't know what's happened, but your girlfriend is controlling you in very negative ways for yourself." I wanted to try a different approach by telling him a little parable about B. F. Skinner, the famous behaviorist who studied classical conditioning. As I started to tell the quick story, in which Skinner conditions a new mouse in his lab by having it push a button for food, my friend immediately drew the conclusion on his own: he was the mouse. It's a unique way to start a conversation, but it allowed him to realize, on his own, that he wasn't in a healthy relationship. That's almost always more palatable for people because, in their minds, they've drawn the conclusion on their own, rather than having to be told by someone else. We really didn't even need the second part of the conversation about his relationship with his girlfriend, because his brain pulled the lesson out of the parable, though we still had it.

He and his girlfriend had an important conversation and are since doing great. Ever since then, I've started collecting parables for different situations. You never know when one can help a friend or family member, and do so in a way that doesn't create resistance. With that said, I want to share one of my favorite parables with you right now. Ironically, it's a parable about parables. When I read this, it locked in the idea that I needed to collect different stories, anecdotes, and parables to be a high-status communicator.

One night Truth, naked and cold, had been turned away from every door in the village. Her nakedness had frightened the people. When Parable found her, she was huddled up in a corner, shivering and hungry. Taking pity on her, Parable gathered her up and took her home. There she dressed Truth in a story and warmed her and sent her out again. This time, clothed in a story, Truth knocked again at the village doors and was readily welcomed into the people's houses. They invited Truth to eat at their tables and warm herself by their fire.

What a perfect parable to remind you to remember parables. People have a habit of rejecting the truth. When you wrap the truth in a story and clothe it with a parable, they accept it. It's a great practice to have a few little stories like that at the ready.

WHAT-IFS

By far, the most common question I get asked about high-status truth is, "What if this is too hard?" I understand why: no one wants to hurt someone they care about. But just remember, if you're coming from a place of love and support, the truth is better for them than speaking falsely.

One tip I tell a lot of my clients to utilize is starting the conversation out by saying, "This is one of the hardest things for me to express. This is going to be difficult for me," or "This has been weighing on my mind for weeks. I can barely sleep, but I just want you to know I'm not comfortable with this." Who is going to reject that, coming from a person they know and trust? No one.

It's going to be hard at first, like training any muscle is, but you will learn to love it. One of my favorite things about high-status truth is you almost become addicted to it. When you get through a challenging conversation with someone and you both emerge still intact, that's an amazing fucking feeling. You'll feel more alert, more alive, and you'll begin to cherish those moments.

If it's hard at first, that's great. You'll build momentum as you go. Just stick with it. Once you get started and run through the different practices and exercises a few times, you'll discover it's actually fun.

And when you're having fun, it becomes very easy to enjoy the next high-status trait—rapport control. Being able to quickly build genuine rapport with people from all walks of life is an invaluable skill that the world's highest-status people have all learned, yet it's wildly understood by most. You're about to become one of the select few people in the world to actually understand how to build true, lasting rapport with anyone. Are you ready? The next page awaits.

Chapter Ten

HIGH-STATUS RAPPORT CONTROL

———

A few years ago, one of my good friends was interested in one of the girls in his social circle. They had both known each other as friends for some time, but he hoped they could become more than that. He finally got her to go out for drinks one night, which led to a second date.

At the end of the second date, my friend leaned in for a good night kiss. She pulled back. It was a total rejection, and he felt like shit about it. In his mind, he had done everything "right" to build rapport. He asked open-ended questions, listened intently, agreed with and approved of her views, and even learned her birthday by the second date. The problem was that he had mistakenly confused being a pushover with building rapport. I am stunned that the majority of rapport-building advice still encourages people to be a subservient mouse to others. Understand: this will not make someone like you. It will make them use you.

Rapport isn't knowing when someone's birthday is, or where they grew up, or what college they went to. It isn't mirroring them physically, despite some insisting it is. It's not even necessarily about finding commonalities, because in finding those commonalities, most come across as needy and try-hard. So, if rapport isn't any of these things, what is it? The simplest definition is that rapport is simply a relationship of responsiveness. When you're in rapport with someone, they respond to your requests, answer your phone calls and texts, and readily do favors for you, just as you do for them. There's responsiveness there between two people.

Rapport control is being able to create rapport with others at a specific speed. Sometimes you can't afford to spend months or years getting to know someone, so you have to hit the fast-forward button. Let's say, for instance, you only have two weeks to close a deal with a business partner or company. You don't have six months to build a long-term relationship. Instead, you have to take all the good parts of a long-term relationship and figure out a way to comfortably piece them together in a much shorter window. That's high-status rapport control.

MORE ON RAPPORT

What else defines strong rapport with someone else? It isn't only a two-way street of responsiveness. Those in rapport will also share a sense of trust. There will be a sense of understanding as well. They will feel comfortable in conversations.

When you're in rapport with someone, you'll find that they open up to you very quickly. I can't tell you how many times I've met someone and, after only five minutes, they start to tell me their entire life story or personal secrets they normally wouldn't tell someone they just met. I was out to dinner recently with a business friend who knows everyone in Hollywood. Our drinks hadn't even arrived before he started revealing all kinds of shocking stories that he definitely shouldn't have been sharing with me. I didn't even ask. It just happened subconsciously as a result of that rapport.

We've already established that rapport is a relationship of responsiveness, not resistance. You'll know you're out of rapport with someone when they resist instead of respond positively to you. The most important key to ensuring there is responsiveness between you and another person is that you approach the interaction with good intentions. We touched on this in the chapter on high-status care-freeness, but it also applies here. If you simply come to any interaction with genuinely heartfelt good intentions, you're not going to encounter resistance, because the other person will feel safe, like they're on your side and you're on theirs. People can always smell what you're cooking, right? If you're not being genuine, people will sniff that out and resist it. You can't fake sincerity.

Along those same lines, if you approach any interaction thinking, it's going to be difficult, or focusing on how you don't like the person, it's doomed to fail. You've got to change that disc in your mind that's playing that kind of negative shit on repeat. Put a new disc in that says, "You know what? This is going to be fun and interesting, and at the very least I'm going to learn something new." That mind-set is so much more powerful.

How else can you avoid resistance? Don't blatantly dis-agree with someone. There is no quicker way to have someone resist everything you say than to totally inval-idate their thoughts or opinions. Someone once asked Robert Downey Jr. what the secret to life is. His response is one of my all-time favorite quotes. He looked at them and said, "Smile, agree, and then do whatever the fuck you were going to do anyway." It's a hilarious response, of course, but it's also great advice. The real genius is in the "smile and agree" part, because those two acts avoid creating resistance. If someone tells you they think you should do something a certain way and you fire back, "Fuck that, you're an idiot. I'm doing it my way," well, that's going to create serious resistance. But if you avoid disagreement by saying, "Your point is well taken" or "I totally see what you're saying," and then continue on your path, you'll maintain a strong sense of rapport. Plus, they may or may not be stunned by your conversational prowess.

There are four specific factors that help avoid resistance and create rapport: shared goals, common enemies, shared experiences, and strong emotions. Let's break them down:

SHARED GOALS

If you ever went to a sleepaway summer camp when you were a kid, you'll probably be able to relate this next example. Even if you didn't, this scenario should still ring true.

Picture two kids—one in Cabin A and the other in Cabin B. During camp, they're on separate teams with the rest of their cabinmates, competing in different games and activities. They're natural enemies, right? They're competing directly against each other to complete the same goal, and probably hurling a few "You suck" or "You're ugly" jabs while they're at it.

Well, what happens when those cabins become one big cabin, and those same kids suddenly find themselves on the same team against a new cabin? Suddenly, the other one doesn't "suck" or look quite so "ugly" anymore. There's an instant shift in rapport, because the two kids share a common goal as teammates.

COMMON ENEMIES

The United States and Mexico don't always get along, but when there's a threat from across the pond, what happens? The two countries band together to protect their lands. It's basically an "us versus them" mentality, and there's a positive response from each side.

SHARED EXPERIENCES

What's one of the most common ways that business professionals create rapport? It isn't through meetings where they share their hopes, goals, or passions. In fact, it's not even in the office. It's on the golf course.

When you're playing a round of golf with someone, you're

sharing an experience together. It creates a stronger bond and sense of rapport, because you're doing something together.

STRONG EMOTIONS

If you have a shared goal or you're fighting together against a shared enemy, there are going to be strong emotions involved. It's naturally provided for you, because you'll both feel a strong desire either to defeat a common enemy or achieve the same goal.

SIGNS OF RAPPORT

In one study, people were asked to make "preference predictions" about people they already knew. In the first group, they were asked to make predictions about people they'd known for ten years. In the other group, they'd known the people for just two years. They also asked the participants how accurate they thought their predictions would be. Everyone in the study predicted they'd be at least 60 percent accurate, regardless if they'd known the person for ten years or two years. So, what were the results?

For people they'd known ten years, the preference predictions were only 36 percent accurate. But it gets stranger.

For people they'd known two years, their preference predictions were higher—42 percent. In my opinion, these people's predictions sucked. If you really tune in and listen to people, and really hear past their words, you can learn so much. The results also spoke loudly about a deep human truth: most of us tell ourselves we mostly know the people around us, but the reality is we don't. To me, that's excellent news. It means there's never been a better time to learn about our friends and family and leverage one of our greatest gifts—our ability to cultivate curiosity.

Cultivating curiosity will help build rapport, because people love it when others are curious about them. We love it when people ask us questions about what we do, where we're going, what we're passionate about, and what's important to us. Almost everyone enjoys being in the spotlight, as long as it's in a comfortable way.

I have a friend who keeps a short list in his head when he meets someone new. He says if he can walk away from a first conversation having learned that person's main goal in life, the thing they fear the most, their greatest passion, the names of their family members, and share at least one inside joke with them, he's as close to them as one of their closest friends in a matter of minutes. It's not a hard-and-fast checklist. That wouldn't be genuine. He just tries to naturally steer the conversation to hit all of those questions.

If you want to know about someone's passion, it's an easy transition to make in conversation. Say you're talking to someone about one of the best players in the NBA, Stephen Curry. You can say, "You know what I love most about Steph Curry? I read his workouts are insane. He shoots 1,500 shots per day. That dude is just so passionate about what he does. What about you? Have you ever had anything in your life that you were that passionate about?" The other person you're talking to might even be taken aback at first, because they've never had anyone show that kind of interest in them before. After a second or two, they'll see your body language isn't leaning in or seeking any kind of approval, and they'll realize, "This could be a great conversation. I'm going to dive in headfirst." In that scenario, you're not being weird or creepy. You're being carefree and high status.

My favorite question to ask people—seriously, you can never go wrong with this—is simply, "So what are you trying to do with your life?" It's so simple, and it cuts right to the heart of it. If you remember the acronym AAJ—aims, ambitions, joys—you'll do well. In fact, that's all you have to talk about to make the conversation a fun, personal and memorable one for the other person.

One of the most common problems I see people run into when trying to build rapport is that they focus too much on the verbal side. They might be in rapport verbally with another person, but the other, nonverbal factors are out of rapport. You don't have to completely mirror someone with the way you sit, stand, and move, but if they have a smaller, quieter energy and speak slowly, you can't come crashing in with a bold, loud energy and rapid pace. You shouldn't be a photographic image of them, but you also shouldn't be crazy different, either. Think about this way: you want the two of you to be like peanut butter and jelly, not peanut butter and jellyfish.

DEEP RAPPORT VERSUS WIDE RAPPORT

These two different types of rapport might sound similar, but they're vastly different. Wide rapport is when your conversation topics with someone include things like your favorite ice cream flavor, your favorite sports teams, the upcoming Halloween party, the time you lost your virginity, and how shit is in the work office. A wide rapport is the ability to talk about a wide variety of topics. It runs across the entire spectrum.

Deep rapport is where someone feels comfortable enough with you that, instead of hitting on a bunch of topics, they want to zero in on one. It's typically personal in nature, but because you both have a deep sense of rapport, you feel comfortable talking about it. Sharing with people your biggest goal in life and what you spend your time thinking about can make you feel vulnerable, so it takes a lot of trust to confide that in someone. You're not going to broadcast something like that around to everyone you meet. Instead, you'll trust the person with good intentions that you have a deep rapport with.

RAPPORT ENERGIZERS

Sometimes you just don't have six months or a year to develop a relationship with someone. You might only have a day or two, or a week or two, so you have to accelerate the rate at which that rapport can grow. To that end, I have seven different rapport energizers to jump-start that acceleration. Just keep in mind to *not* use all seven simultaneously on one person. That would be complete overkill. It's like a buffet. Pick one or two that work best in a given situation.

BEN FRANKLIN TRICK

Back when in the late 1700s when Ben Franklin was seeking reelection as a delegate in the Pennsylvania legislature, a younger rival candidate emerged. Franklin wanted to take him under his wing and groom him for the future, but the new guy had no interest in that.

Franklin asked around and found out that the guy had an impressive collection of rare and valuable books. Franklin, being a voracious reader himself, wrote him a letter asking to borrow one book in particular. Franklin asked to borrow the book for six weeks and promised to return it on time.

The rival legislator was flattered by this request, so he sent the book. Franklin received the book, put it on his desk, and didn't touch it for the entire six weeks before he returned it on time, as promised. At the next legislative gathering, instead of ignoring him, the younger guy approached Franklin and struck up a pleasant conversation. The two remained close for the rest of their lives. What happened?

There's a psychological principle called the commitment and consistency bias, and it states that when we act a certain way toward someone, whether it's positive or negative, we take meaning from that action about how we feel about that person. Simply receiving a favor from someone will actually make them like you and trust you more.

CONFESSIONS

This one comes courtesy of Warren Buffet, who is very quietly a master of rapport. Every year, Buffet writes a letter to all the Berkshire Hathaway stockholders detailing the previous year, the current state of the company, and what lies ahead. Every single shareholder looks forward to that letter, because it's the one time of year they all get to hear directly from him.

For the last several decades, Buffet has opened every letter not with an accomplishment or milestone, but with a confession. He confesses something that *didn't* go as planned for the business in the previous year. Why would he do this? He's Warren fucking Buffet. He could brag about any number of accomplishments in any year.

By offering a confession, he's being honest. When you read something like that, you think, "He may be really successful, but he's also honest. He admitted a mistake. We all make mistakes." Making a confession to someone brings them closer to you, and can often turn an adversary into an ally.

SHARING A SECRET

Back in the early nineteenth century, Napoleon Bonaparte was the face of power in France. But it was his right-hand man, Charles Maurice de Talleyrand-Périgord, who proved invaluable. Talleyrand was an expert conversationalist who could get others to reveal their feelings and ideas without even knowing it.

He had one trick in particular that he used repeatedly to his benefit. When with another foreign diplomat or high-ranking official in private, Talleyrand would often blurt out what would appear to be a big secret. It was usually just something he made up, but he would pay attention to the other people's reactions, which would give him information.

The obvious benefit was that he could gauge reactions, but there was also a secondary benefit: people would feel compelled to share a secret with him. Sharing secrets is an incredible way to build rapport. Talleyrand was a politician, one that even those closest to him didn't fully trust. I don't want you to go around lying to everyone you meet, just to learn some of their secrets.

Just keep a few personal secrets about yourself at the ready for whenever you might need them. This is why people bond so easily over gossip.

MERE-EXPOSURE EFFECT

When humans are simply exposed to something more than a few times, they tend to start responding more positively to it. "Familiarity breeds contempt" is an old saying, but it's only proven true after hundreds and hundreds of repeated exposures. If the exposure isn't overwhelming, studies show that makes us like something more.

A study was done that showed people normal pictures of themselves, as well as reverse images of themselves. Almost unanimously, people preferred the reverse image. Why is that? We've all seen ourselves in the mirror our entire lives, so that's the image of ourselves we've seen most often. It's the mere-exposure effect.

So how can you apply this to your own high-status rapport control? One of the best ways is through writing letters. You remember what those look like, right? Not an e-mail, not a text, not a Snapchat—a handwritten letter that you physically mail to someone. There's a deeper impact when someone receives a letter, so you'll find yourself on their mind in a meaningful way, instead of in their computer's trash can.

John F. Kennedy understood the importance of letters better than most. People close to him said, "While the rest of the world carries on senseless conversations, JFK would be writing letters." Who was he writing them to? To all kinds of people, some of whom you'd expect more than others. He understood it was important to be constantly remain on people's radars by keeping in touch with them. If someone isn't exposed to you on a consistent basis, you can still cultivate the power of the mere-exposure effect.

RECOGNITION

There is almost no better way to light someone up and truly make them want to respond to you than by simply recognizing them uniquely. No one does this anymore. It's a basic communication skill that Dale Carnegie was teaching 100 years ago, but it's almost extinct now. You can help change that.

When you meet someone, aside from filing away their name and face, make a mental note of one unique thing about them. I try to do this whenever I meet someone, so that the next time we see each other, I can ask them about that specific thing.

This simple gesture will illustrate to the other person that they were memorable to you, which is a genuine way of recognizing them.

RECIPROCITY

We do unto others what they do unto us. That's the definition of reciprocity, and it goes for both positive and negative interactions. If someone does a disservice to you, you're going to feel compelled to give them a taste of disservice back. But if someone does something uniquely kind to you, you're going to want to do the same for them.

When you're using reciprocity to energize and accelerate rapport, one of the most effective methods is gift-giving. I don't mean just going down to the local store and buying a Starbucks gift card with no emotion or thought. Instead, combine recognition and reciprocity.

As an example, let's say I meet someone and the one unique fact I save in my mind about them is that they absolutely love Dungeons & Dragons. They can't get enough of it, right? Instead of a generic Starbucks gift card, I get them a rare Dungeons & Dragons collectible. That's going to create *a lot* more reciprocity.

BREAK RAPPORT

Full disclosure: this seventh and final rapport energizer is an advanced one. Make yourself comfortable with the first six we've highlighted before you try this one.

Breaking rapport, or at least the *idea* of breaking rapport, seems counterintuitive, right? We've spent all this time focusing on ways to build rapport, so why would we ever want to break it? Interestingly enough, it's actually the fastest way to build rapport with someone.

Breaking rapport is simply teasing someone, or making fun of them in a friendly way. It might seem like you're pushing them away, but when it's done in a playful way, it actually builds rapport. Everyone has friends like this. Guys love to give each other shit. Girls do, too. Think about your best friends. Do you have inside jokes with them? Of course. Do you make fun of each other but have a good time doing it? Absolutely.

If you meet someone and within a minute you're making fun of each other in a playful way, what happens to your sense of rapport with that person? They are embodying the traits, signals, and characteristics of the people you've been closest with your entire life, so you begin to feel that same rapport with them. This is one of the high-level rapport hacks we teach at my seminars, and the results are consistently stunning.

WHAT-IFS

Let's review some of the common questions I get asked about high-status rapport control before we wrap up this chapter.

WE'RE DISAGREEING

Look, sometimes you're going to do everything you can to avoid resistance and create a relationship of responsiveness, yet you and the other person will still disagree.

Don't sweat it. It's actually great, because you can easily reframe the entire situation.

All of you have to do is say something like, "You know what? We disagree so much, we're like Starsky and Hutch." Or if you're a woman talking with another woman, something like, "We disagree about everything. We're just like Lucy and Ethel." Boom—it changes the entire dynamic.

You can use any well-known character tandem, as long as they were great friends who argued a lot. It will reframe the rapport in your friend's mind as the same thing.

I'M TRYING TOO HARD

If you get the sense that you're trying too hard for rapport and it's not working, don't panic. In this situation, the first step is to put all of the rapport control energizers on hold for the time being.

Instead, you're going to first take a deep breath and lean back. Remember, when in doubt, lean out. Focus on your own body language. Just taking yourself out of the moment briefly with a few deep breaths will help you develop rapport more effectively than anything else you can say or do in that situation. Just lean back and let the situation come to you.

PRACTICE MAKES PERFECT

Rapport control, like every other high-status signal in this book, is a muscle that you'll have to train. You've learned the behaviors and signs of rapport, as well as the energizers that can accelerate rapport control.

Now, you've just got to practice them. Remember not to spray all seven energizers across conversations like a machine gun. Just focus on one or two, and pepper them in when talking to someone. If you do that, you're going to have the power to rapidly build rapport with anyone in no time.

When you combine that skill with high-status charisma, the next high-status trait, the results are outstanding—enough to make your competition bright green with envy.

Chapter Eleven

HIGH-STATUS CHARISMA

———

When the first iPhone was being built, the original plan called for it to have a plastic screen like the iPod. But Steve Jobs wanted something more elegant than plastic. He wanted glass. Of course, it had to be strong glass that wouldn't scratch or crack easily. He put the word out and eventually got connected with a CEO who supposedly had just the type of glass Jobs was looking for.

After a series of back-and-forth periods of phone tag, Jobs finally invited the CEO of Corning, Inc., out to Apple headquarters to meet with him. The CEO told Jobs about a new type of glass that had taken decades to develop, called Gorilla Glass. Up until that point, there had been no need or use for glass that strong. Jobs remained unconvinced, so he started explain to the CEO how glass is made. As Jobs was drawing away on a whiteboard, the CEO started to get annoyed. Finally, he stood up and said, "Can you shut up for a second and just let me teach you some science?"

Jobs was taken aback. No one spoke to him that way. As he slumped back in his chair, the Corning CEO took his place at the whiteboard and began a lengthy tutorial on the chemistry behind glass. Once he finished, the first thing Jobs said was, "I want as much Gorilla Glass as you can possibly make in the next six months."

"We don't have the capacity for that," the CEO replied. "None of our plants even make the glass right now." Jobs didn't panic. He didn't get angry or discouraged. He simply replied, "Don't be afraid. You can do this. Get your mind around it. You can do this." Of course, the rest is history: the glass is produced, the iPhone explodes into a billion-dollar industry, and the way our species communicates is forever changed. But it never would have happened if Jobs hadn't had high-status charisma.

What defines charisma? What is it? Ask twenty people and you'll probably get twenty different answers. Allow me to simplify it. What creates charisma is a sense of certainty. Whether it's a guy who's the life of the party, a historical figure who led a revolution, a speaker onstage getting the crowd fired up, or the coach of a championship team, the common thread among all of them is a sense of certainty. They might not always be right, but they never hesitate. Other people feed on this. In a world full of drifting leaves, the charismatic man or woman is the wind.

If Jobs had hesitated at all during his interactions with Corning, Inc., it never would have happened. What if he had said, "Um, OK, what about nine months instead of six? Or is there another option? Maybe something similar to Gorilla Glass?"

TRAITS OF CHARISMA

If you were writing up the recipe for high-status charisma, there are three main ingredients that are needed for the dish: certainty in motion, decisiveness, and passion. Let's look at each one.

CERTAINTY IN MOTION

Think of three charismatic people you know. They can be close friends, coworkers, even celebrities. It doesn't matter. Do you consider any of them to be hesitant people? Of course not. I don't even need to know the three people you thought of, and I still know the answer is, without a doubt, no.

Certainty in motion means you are doing things on the path to your high-status destiny. Everything you do has a certainty to it. When you're in a business meeting, you're certain. When you're having dinner with someone, you're certain. You are certain in the things you're saying in these different settings, because you know you're on a destined path. Other people not only sense that, but they're attracted to it.

I was building a company a few years ago that no longer exists now. That along should give you an idea of where this story is heading. Over the years, any company or business endeavor I've had that was successful came from an idea that I was certain about. The ones where I said, "This is a great idea. I am *certain* about this. We'll figure it out as we go, but let's just get this thing fucking started." Those ideas always thrive.

The ones that fail, like the particular company I just mentioned, come from the less certain ideas. Instead of being raring to go, I say to myself, "This is a great idea, but let's make sure we take our time in the planning process, secure the capital, and do the research." Those ideas are fucked from the start, so it's no surprise that six months after starting the company, I shut it down. By approaching that company with hesitation, I forgot what people actually value—certainty. People don't care that everything is 100 percent perfect all the time. They don't want a mistake-free world. What they actually want from their leaders is certainty.

There was a fascinating study done on certainty using, all of things, a jaywalker. They had a guy stand at a busy street corner full of other pedestrians. The idea was to have him jaywalk and observe the reactions of other people. In the first setup, the guy would stand at the corner and, when no cars were coming, would look once quickly to make sure it was safe, and then walk certainly and confidently across the street.

In the second setup, the guy did the same thing except he hesitated. He put his foot out into the street, but pulled it back. He looked right, then left, then right again. After a few seconds, he finally walked across. The results of the study were pretty staggering. Seven times as many people followed the guy in the certain, confident walk of the first setup as opposed to the hesitant walk of the second setup.

I'll share another quick story to highlight the power of certainty in motion. Before Jerry Weintraub was the Emmy Award-winning legend he is now, he tried to get in touch with an actor who was starring in a Broadway play. At that point, Weintraub didn't have the credentials to be able to walk freely backstage, so he had to get a little creative.

After he snuck his way backstage, he still had to get past security to get to the area where the dressing rooms for the actors and actresses were located. As he looked around for something to help his cause, he noticed a clipboard. Perfect.

As Weintraub walked up to the security guard, his plan began to take shape. "How's your night going?" Weintraub asked while he slapped him on the shoulder. "Good," he replied. "How was your training? Has your training been adequate to the tasks that you've been assigned here?" Weintraub continued. "Yeah, I was trained pretty well," the guy replied. "Good to hear. We've had our eye on you and we think you're doing a great job. Keep it up." Weintraub slapped him on the shoulder again and walked right by. It's a funny story, but it so clearly illustrates the power of certainty. Weintraub later said, "If you act like you know exactly what you're doing, people won't really bother you."

I was teaching one of my higher-end workshops in 2016 for about thirty guys. The tickets were $2,500 apiece for the two-day workshop, and we covered a lot of great stuff. But a few guys approached me toward the end of the second day during a break with a proposal: eight of them were going to pay me $5,000 each for an additional day of just straight questions and answers. My initial reaction was shock. I'm the one that was supposed to be making the offers, not them. I just thought it was so cool these guys pitched that idea, but I didn't act uncertain about it. I practiced my high-status state control, remained calm, considered the offer and came back to the guys with my conditions for the Q and A.

One of my mentors taught me the importance of acting as if there are no limits to your abilities. When you have certainty in motion, you get a positive response. Your brain remembers that. If you haven't been acting as if there are no limits to your abilities, it's not surprising that you haven't become the most charismatic version of yourself yet. You've just been training in the wrong direction, but it's easy to flip that.

DECISIVENESS

Let's be honest—today's world is fucking flooded with indecisive people. Nothing screams "don't trust or follow me" more than indecisiveness. There's a great quote that captures this idea: "If you want no one to ever say a single bad word about you, say nothing, do nothing, and be nothing." Indecisive people, by not making a decision and not being certain, avoid all possible negative outcomes and, by default, all responsibility.

A charismatic person is going to make an immediate decision that will sometimes be right. When people take their time to gather data or write out a pros and cons list, do you trust them? No, because in your mind you're thinking, "They weren't sure of their decision. How can I be sure of them?" People value quick, decisive decision-making.

Everyone knows about Julius Caesar, but not everyone knows that he was kidnapped by a band of pirates in his youth. How would most people handle that situation? How would you handle being a chained prisoner of a team of sword-wielding pirates, with no Instagram or Snapchat to send out a distress signal? Caesar thrived in it because he was brash and decisive. As the pirates debated among themselves how much to hold Caesar for ransom, Caesar implored them to ask for at least three times more. The pirates took a liking to such boldness and, as they got to know him more, developed an appreciation for him. Caesar made a point of telling them, "When I get free, I just want you to know that I'm going to commandeer a ship, find you, and kill each and every one of you." The pirates all had a great laugh at this, but the last laugh was on them. Caesar's ransom was eventually paid, he was freed, and, upon returning to Rome, he got a ship and pursued the pirates. When he found them, he crucified all of them. Now that's an *extreme* form of decisiveness, but it damn sure was charismatic.

Another great story on decisiveness comes from one of my personal mentors, Dan Peña. He's known as the "50 Billion Dollar Man" because between him and the people he's mentored, they've created more than $50 billion of value over the years. Peña's most successful student, at least from a financial perspective, is Rick Scott, the governor of Florida. The two first met back in 1993 when Scott was a transaction lawyer for Peña. After a while, Scott noticed the sheer amount of money Peña was making on all of his deals, and realized he was getting the short end of the stick. Scott asked him how he could make similar money, so Peña suggested going into health care and laid out a plan how to do it. Scott didn't stop to consider it, or weigh his options, or put together a pro-con list. He walked out of the room and dove into the plan headfirst. A few years later, Scott owned a health care company worth $17 billion. He was certainty in motion and he was decisive.

PASSION

Everyone knows that being passionate is important. This isn't groundbreaking information, yet how few people do you know who swim daily in the deep end of their passion? We've all been told our entire lives to have passion, yet no one cultivates their passion. I have people come up to me every day and thank me for something I said or did that changed their lives by lighting the fire deep inside of them.

Many confide that, before that crucial moment in their life, they had been a drifting leaf instead of a purposeful, forceful wind. Why do so many choose to stay treading in the shallow waters of their life? One major reason is they lack a high-status destiny. They might have a path in life that was given to them by someone else, whether it's parents, friends, or family. We all invest so much more in the things we choose for ourselves. You know what you love and what excites you, so if you've built a life around something else, you're going to drift and you're going to lack interest.

The other major reason people drift through life is because they're easily distracted. Since they don't like what they're doing, every little thing they encounter in life becomes a distraction. Calling it a distraction at this point is almost a misnomer, since many are actively looking to be distracted by something...anything. Funny story—technology was actually created to make lives easier. The idea was to take menial jobs and tasks out of human hands, so we could enjoy more recreation, leisure, and travel. Well, that's definitely not happened. Technology has stressed people out more than ever. It distracts us and has ruined our attention spans. It's a nightmare. Worst of all, people live in environments that are full of distractions—cell phones, TVs, music streaming, you name it. So many people are drifting and distracted, instead of passionate.

When we meet someone who is truly passionate, we're like, "Holy shit! Who are you and where have you been all my life?" We find that quality immediately attractive. We're drawn to it. My challenge to you is this: Will you become that rare person, that one in a thousand, who isn't dabbling and distracted but instead is attacking their passion and purpose with every ounce of vigor you have? I strongly encourage you to say yes now, and give yourself this life-changing gift.

Leonardo DiCaprio is a perfect example of someone who's incredibly passionate about what he does. People who don't understand that will say he's lucky, or he was just born to be an actor, but we know that's not true. His longtime friend, Tobey Maguire, learned this at a young age. Before DiCaprio became a living legend, he was an up-and-coming actor just like Maguire, and the two would often compete for the same roles. One day, DiCaprio was in the car with his mom when he spotted Maguire standing off to the side of a street. He had his mom stop the car.

"Hey man, you're Tobey, right?" he said. "Yeah, hey. You're Leo, right?" Maguire replied. "Come on, get in. Let's go," DiCaprio said. Maguire was a little hesitant. "What do you mean?" "You're my friend. Let's go get some ice cream or something."

Maguire learned early on that when DiCaprio decides someone is going to be his friend, that's the end of the story. He decides who his friends will be. That's how he operates. DiCaprio is not a lucky success story. He's a man of purpose and passion.

Here's the beautiful thing about passion: it can take any form. Fantasy football, brush painting, online coding—anything that truly crosses the threshold from an interest to a healthy obsession can become your passion.

BUILDING HIGH-STATUS CHARISMA

I know I sound like a broken record at this point, but I'm going to say it again anyway: charisma, like all of the other high-status signals in this book, is a muscle that you must train. There are three specific exercises that I want you start practicing.

CHARISMA MODE

For thirty seconds at a time, I want you to turn up the juices and go into what you consider to be your most charismatic mode. Be as certain, decisive, and passionate as you can be for thirty seconds, whether you're walking down the street, ordering food at a restaurant, or just walking to the break room at work.

Do this three separate times today. Don't put it off until tomorrow or next week. As always, take note of the responses you get from people. I promise you're going to find they respond to you better than they ever have before. You'll start to build charisma momentum.

MAGNIFY POSITIVITY

One thing all charismatic people have in common is an ability to forget negativity and magnify positivity. My friend, the "Three-Foot Giant" Sean Stephenson, has said that you should only listen to predictions that empower you. I agree. I remember one of my first organized basketball games, when I was fourteen years old. I made seven three-pointers in the game, which was more than I had ever made before. After the game, I looked at the stat sheet and saw I finished seven-for-seventeen on three-point shot attempts. In my mind, I had only taken—and made—seven three-pointers. My brain had literally forgotten the other ten misses. I only remembered the ball going through the net.

Moving forward, I want you to start saving the compliments you get. A lot of times people brush off compliments. Don't do that. A compliment is a gift for your charisma. Take it, save it, and let it feed your already-growing charisma.

For this exercise, I want you to write down ten specific compliments that you remember receiving. Keep a running list somewhere that you can readily access any time you're not feeling great. Each time you read a compliment, it will provide a nice little confidence boost.

LIST OF LIKES

You'll need to set aside some time for this, but don't skip it just because it takes a little longer. You're going to build another list, preferably in the same journal or document as the compliment list, but this time of fifty things you like about yourself.

This will be challenging for some. The media trains us to focus on what's wrong, not what's right or what's positive. The good news is that you and I both know you already understand how to focus on one thing more than another. Now, we're going to change that focus to something far more interesting—the best things about you.

CHARISMA IS CONTROLLABLE

Charisma is widely misunderstood. Most people think it's some kind of ungraspable, indefinable quality. That's bullshit. You now know the qualities and traits that define charisma. You know how to start building your own high-status charisma. You know how to behavior-ally demonstrate charisma, not just talk about it. You've got this.

There are two high-status traits we haven't stripped down to their bare essence yet, and these two traits have the power to unlock enormous results in your life that you can't even begin to imagine. You think you're ready for such transformation? Turn the page and I'll show you the hard core steps and secrets most teachers and gurus are too afraid or ashamed to share with you.

Chapter Twelve

HIGH-STATUS STYLE

———

I've mentioned the 50 Billion Dollar Man Dan Peña a few times in this book, but let me tell you a funny story about the first time he and I sat down to talk. I was at his eight-day seminar in the summer of 2015 at his castle in Scotland. That's right—the guy lives in a castle. Not just a really big, nice house with twenty-eight rooms that he calls his "castle," but a real-life, honest-to-God castle.

When you walk onto the property, the first thing you see is the eighteen-hole golf course he built on the grounds. Then you hear the roar of an engine. What type of car, you ask? Hard to say. It could be his Ferrari, or maybe his Aston Martin, or perhaps his Rolls-Royce. It depends on the day. As you make your walk across the property, which takes twenty-five minutes to cover, you begin to feel a sense of wealth and opportunity flow through you. It's an inspiring place.

As Dan and I sat down for our meeting, I told him about the goals for my company and what I hoped to accomplish in the future. The conversation was going well until he got to my suit. "Wait. When you go on stage, traveling, speaking, coaching, you're wearing that suit?" For once in my life, I didn't know what to say.

Quick side note—suits were required for the entire eight-day seminar, except for a short break each day, which I usually spent at the gym working out. For me, the work attire of choice for the last few years has been board shorts and flip-flops. Shit, I don't even wear a shirt most of the time because I work from my house, and I want to be comfortable. Wearing a suit all day, every day was unusual for me. In preparation for Peña's seminar, I went out and got what I thought was a sharp, tailored Hugo Boss suit for like $2,500. He wasn't impressed.

"That's really what you wear?" Peña asked. "Yeah, of course," I said. "Why? Is something wrong?" "Yeah, everything's wrong," he replied. "You can't wear that suit." Again, I asked him why—I had to get the most out of my one-on-one time with him.

"You only get one shot at a first impression. I assure you, when people see you in that suit, they're not going to be impressed. What you need is a suit that demonstrates your success. You need a Tom Ford suit. It'll cost you five or six grand, and people will respond to you completely differently. If they're already responding well, you have no idea how much easier it'll get with the right suit."

Interesting, I thought. Then I asked him if anything else needed to change. "Take your earrings out and take the bracelets off. You look like you smoke pot."

"And," he added, "get a fucking haircut." The great Dan Peña does *not* pull punches, and I love him for that. I agreed with all of his suggestions...except the haircut. That's just one thing I'll never budge on.

WHY STYLE MATTERS

Most people seem to understand that style is important, but it's amazing how many people just don't put any conscious thought into how they will present themselves to the world. I read a quote recently that went, "A really high-class, tailored suit on a man is the equivalent of a tight black dress and six-inch heels on a woman." Both of those examples provide powerful mental images, but keep in mind that there's more to style than just clothing.

You have control over the first impression you make on others with your style, and you don't have to be stuck in what you used to wear or what you see other people wearing. There's a very specific, three-step path I want you to take with high-status style. First, high-status style captivates attention. Second, after captivating that attention, it signals high status. And third, it makes you unforgettable. It has to happen in that order. If you can't captivate someone's attention, you won't have a chance to signal your high status or become unforgettable.

THE POWER OF STYLE

If your local mall has an Apple Store, I already know it's the busiest of all the stores in it. People used to go to malls for clothes. Now they go for the Apple Store. The Apple Store can trace its roots all the way back to 1970s and Mike Markkula, one of the early investors in Apple. Markkula wrote a short, one-page paper that highlighted the three principles for the company's marketing philosophy: empathy, focus, impute. The goal was to connect with the customer (empathy), eliminate all other distractions (focus), and leave the biggest impact possible (impute).

In his paper, Markkula wrote, "People do judge a book by its cover. We may have the best products and software, but if we present in a slipshod manner, they'll be perceived as slipshod. If we present them in a creative, professional manner, then we will impute the desired qualities inside the experience of the user." That stuck with Steve Jobs for a long time. He spent months and months building different prototypes for the store before it ever saw the inside of a mall. He would build practice models inside a private garage near Apple headquarters and invite people like Larry Ellison, the billionaire CEO of Oracle, to come visit and offer advice. It was critical to Jobs that the store impute the right message. He knew the store would "become the most powerful physical expression of the brand."

We've seen the power of first impression throughout history. Renaissance philosopher Niccolò Machiavelli wrote in his treatise *The Prince*, "Men judge by their eyes." Baltasar Gracián, a Spanish philosopher and writer, once wrote, "The truth is generally seen, rarely heard." In today's society, attention spans are shorter than ever, so you don't really have the time to set the right impression over a dinner or happy-hour drinks. You will be judged on appearance, and it will happen in a matter of seconds.

Why do first impressions weigh so heavily? One reason is something called the halo effect. What this means is that, when you make a high-status great first impression on someone, they attribute many other positive qualities to you, even if you haven't demonstrated any of them. The halo effect is more commonly applied in terms of physical attractiveness, where more physically attractive people are seen as smarter, stronger, and more successful. Halo effect studies are fascinating. One was done on Canadian federal elections, and it found that attractive candidates received two-and-a-half more votes than unattractive candidates. When they asked voters about this, almost three-quarters of them denied that physical appearance had any bearing on their vote. The halo effect was there, but they didn't even realize it was influencing their thoughts and behaviors.

The other reason is perseverance of the first impression. There's something called belief perseverance, which suggests that even in the face of conflicting evidence, people don't change their first impressions. If we ever do change our minds and decide to reevaluate someone, we consider that an exception to the rule. We mostly refuse to change our initial impression of someone because that would mean admitting we were wrong, and we don't like doing that. First impressions matter: you've got to make a good one.

CATCHING ATTENTION

The first step in high-status style is catching someone's

attention. If you can't do that, you won't be able to signal your high status or make yourself unforgettable. Without attention, there's no influence, and without influence, there's no opportunity to build.

Remember when Björk showed up at the 2001 Academy Awards wearing a swan around her neck? That's a prime example of trying too hard to captivate attention. If you find yourself wearing a swan dress, you've gone too far. So how do you gain attention without trying too hard? Simple—the incongruity theory.

The incongruity theory means you're going to be incongruent, or incompatible, with a specific environment, and that will make you stand out. If you walked into a restaurant and saw nine people wearing blue shirts and one person wearing a red shirt, who would stand out? The person in red, right? You just have to be slightly incongruent with your environment. If there's a particular bar you frequent, take note of how people dress. Figure out how you can dress differently to stand out, while not going to the extreme of wearing a swan around your neck. If everyone is wearing a cheap suit, try to invest in a nicer one. Personally, I never wear blue jeans. They're uncomfortable and, honestly, I don't like how they look. Everyone else in the world wears jeans though, so I get a few benefits by choosing not to wear them. I'm captivating attention by being slightly incongruent, and I'm happy because board shorts are way more comfortable.

Someone who totally got incongruity theory was David Ogilvy, the advertising executive from the late twentieth century who served as the inspiration for *Mad Men*'s Don Draper. Before he became the king of Madison Avenue, Ogilvy was originally from Scotland. He became known around New York City for wearing a full-length, flowing black cape with a scarlet lining around his suit. Sometimes he wore kilts to black tie events. He owned one of the first Rolls-Royces in New York City. The guy just embraced incongruity theory.

ATTENTION ENVIRONMENTS

Before you move on to signaling high status, I want you to do two quick exercises.

EXERCISE NO. 1

Ask yourself what the three most important environments in your life now, or potentially in the future, are. So, to use myself as an example, I could say onstage, my offices, and the gym as my three most important environments. For someone else it could be work, networking events, and a specific bar. The answer will be different for everyone. Think of your three most important environments.

EXERCISE NO. 2

What is the one thing in each of those environments that mostly everyone wears that isn't necessary or could be made better? Take your three answers and, boom, you have a new rule for each of your environments. If your answer for the first environment is blue jeans, then never wear blue jeans in that environment ever again. Plus, now you have the fun of picking out something new and more badass to wear.

SIGNAL HIGH STATUS

Branding is a powerful tool. You know this if you've ever taken an advertising class, or even just watched TV commercials. Apple's financial boom wasn't directly tied to iPod sales in the early 2000s. But because people loved the experience, packaging, and performance of the iPod, it led to increased sales across Apple's entire product line. Along the same lines, when the sandwich chain Subway changed its slogan to "Eat Fresh," it rebranded itself as a healthy dining option. The reality is that Subway still serves chicken bacon ranch, meatball, and all kinds of other shit that's not healthy at all, but the branding says otherwise.

We can generate the same effect with you. If you can make a high-status first impression with your own personal branding, people are going to attribute other positive qualities to you as well. Think about this way: Remember the first day of school you ever went to? Everyone got their own cubby with their name on it for storing your jacket, backpack, and anything else under the sun. Guess what? Our brains work just like cubbies, storing different information into different areas. When we make an assessment of someone's first impression, we're deciding whether they're high, neutral, or low status; someone you want to date or sleep with; and on and on and on. We have all these different cubbies, and again, because of belief perseverance, once something goes in a certain cubby, it usually stays there. The goal is to make sure your first impression goes in the correct cubby.

How can you do that? Start by looking to celebrities. Actually, let me clarify: start by looking at celebrities. They're constantly surrounded by a team of experts whose only job is to make them look amazing.

SIGNALING EXERCISE NO. 1

Start by answering this question: Who are three celebrities that have a style you love? It can actors, actresses, online personalities—it's up to you. If you love their style, put them on the list.

SIGNALING EXERCISE NO. 2

Which of the three celebrities on your list screams "high status" to you? All of them might seem high status to you, but which one just is the most powerful?

SIGNALING EXERCISE NO. 3

What do their wardrobes and outfits usually include? List everything you've seen them wear. Photos can certainly help with that. Follow up that list with this question: What do their wardrobes and outfits *not* include?

If you combine the results of these three quick exercises, you'll now have a new style to model. For instance, if you're a guy, and you chose Ryan Gosling as your celebrity who screams "high status," and you make a list of everything he wears after doing some online research, you'll have a list of the things you will and won't wear. That list becomes your brand.

There's no reason you have to be stuck as the kind of person your parents or teachers said you were when you were younger. You have the power to decide who you're going to be. Are you going to let other people determine what kind of first impression you're going to make on the rest of the world for the rest of your damn life? Or are you going to let your own purpose, path, and goals in life determine what kind of first impression you'll make?

BECOMING UNFORGETTABLE

There are two big keys to making sure no one forgets you. The first is simply making sure your clothing fits you well. Big, baggy, wrinkled clothes will not be remembered. Wear clothes that contour positively to the size and shape of your body. The trick to ensuring this is getting all of your clothing tailored. I mean it—all of your clothing, even T-shirts. It will make a $10 white V-neck look like a $100 T-shirt. No one tailors all of their clothing, so if you do, you'll stand out as incongruent.

The second key is imprint triggers, which are little accessories that give you an added appeal to your look. They shouldn't be over the top, like Chris Tucker's blonde hair in *The Fifth Element*, but they shouldn't be too subtle, either. The rule of thumb is that when someone looks at you for three or four seconds, they should be able to see the imprint. You should have two or three imprint triggers on you at a given time. Remember the saying, "What stands out, gets in."

There's also an interesting phenomenon known as the availability-misweighting bias, which basically states that we give more value to things that are more easily recalled by our memory. With high-status style, we're going to make you unforgettable, so that when you interview for that job with nine other candidates, you'll be the one the boss remembers later that night when they go home.

UNFORGETTABLE EXERCISE NO. 1

What accessories does your celebrity model wear? Make a list of everything you see. It will give you an idea of how to make your own style unforgettable.

UNFORGETTABLE EXERCISE NO. 2

What accessory do you really like that you've seen someone else wear, but could never picture yourself wearing? Don't worry. You don't actually have to wear it. I just want your brain to start thinking outside its normal scope. Get out of the comfort zone you've had yourself stuck in for years.

YOUR NEXT STEPS

Here's what I want you to do: stop reading and go get what you need to test out your new high-status style. Don't put it off until the weekend. Get it done today. It all starts with a baby step. Maybe it's ordering something online, or changing your facial hair, or simply getting rid of any existing clothes in your closet you *never* wear. I don't expect you to go out and buy an entire new wardrobe in one shopping trip, but get enough to at least test out one new outfit. As always, observe and notice how people respond to you differently.

The first impression you will make will be so much more powerful. People of the opposite sex will respond to you more easily. People at work will start to follow your lead and respect you more. Even your family and friends will truly take your advice to heart. Style is one of the most important high-status signals, so don't waste this opportunity.

BALLIN' ON A BUDGET

Let me make this absolutely clear: high-status style has nothing to do with how much money you make. I'm fortunate because I can comfortably afford more expensive suits, but you build an entire new wardrobe for next to nothing.

H&M and Forever 21 are the best options if you're in the younger demographic. If you feel like those stores aren't for you, there are two other options—vintage and thrift stores, and the Internet. Thrift stores are a gold mine. Let's say you find a jacket that sold for $500 twenty years ago, but is now available for $10. It will cost less than $5 to get it professionally tailored. You can build an incredibly wardrobe for less than $100 simply by buying items at thrift stores and getting them tailored.

The Internet is always a viable option as well. Sales pop up seemingly every hour, every day. Two of the better sites I've seen are Jack Threads for men and Poshmark for women. You can also get a serious jump start on rebuilding your wardrobe by simply getting rid of old clothes you don't want anymore.

Keep in mind the specific traits of high-status style we highlighted in this chapter, and work off of your answers to the exercise questions. You'll be able to build a new wardrobe and a new brand of style that reflects your high-status self in no time—and for minimal money.

That's a pretty good combination, isn't it? Damn right. And it brings us to the twelfth and final honest signal: environment. Have you ever been surrounded by people who bring you down and wished there was just more energy and positivity around you? Maybe you even began to imagine how much further along you'd be if you'd had surroundings that truly supported you and your goals. What if I told you that getting that type of environment only takes three simple steps?

What comes next isn't a chapter, but a workshop—a workshop that you'll look back on one day and think, "That was the day my eyes truly opened to what I was capable of. That was the day I made the decision to get the life of my dreams, and my goodness, I'm so glad I did." Let the games begin.

Chapter Thirteen

HIGH-STATUS ENVIRONMENT

—

Think about this particular scenario I'm about to describe and whether you've found yourself in it before. You've set a goal for yourself to go to the gym every day after work, let's say around 6:00 p.m. You've been doing pretty well for the first few days, but on the fourth day someone—a significant other, a roommate, anyone—stops you and says, "Come on, skip the gym. We haven't hung out like normal in a while. Let's watch Netflix or *Game of Thrones*." What would you do in that situation? Don't tell me what I want to hear. Be honest with yourself. If you're like most, the temptation will suffocate your will power, and you'll dissolve the developing gym habit. But hey, at least you'd know what was going on with the Targaryens and Lannisters!

It's understandable. Most people in that situation would think the other person is just being a good friend seeking company. Here's the harsh reality. While they might be a good person, their actions are creating an environment that is pulling you down. You might have every intention of getting into the shape you want, yet their presence has made it harder for you to do that. That's an environment that feeds low-status behaviors and habits. A high-status environment is one that raises you up and *doesn't* pull you down.

Can you imagine all the different areas of your life where you would be stronger, faster, quicker, smarter, and better if you were in an environment that raised you up and challenged you constantly? How many of your ideas would have set sail without stormy weather looming overhead? Most people have forgotten that they can actually make this happen for themselves. They can design an environment that doesn't have negativity, or complaining, or people who invalidate their intentions to rise, grow, and evolve as a human being. Imagine the freedom and power you'd feel to pursue your dreams with no restraints.

When it comes to environment, there are three types of people: drifters, victims, and leaders.

- **Drifters** allow their environment to take shape by accident. There's no purpose, rhyme, or reason to the environment they choose to live in, so whatever happens is fine with them.

- **Victims** have things in their environment that, consciously and unconsciously, prime and trigger negative emotions like anger, frustration, worry and depression. They've either on purpose or by accident allowed an environment to take shape around them that pulls them down.

- **Leaders**, on the other hand, deliberately and consciously create an environment that raises them up. It has things that prime and trigger positive, joyful, resourceful, and excited responses. The fact that you've made it this far in the book means you're already a leader. Now it's time for us to build an environment for you that represents that.

LAW OF ENVIRONMENTAL EXPOSURE

When Julius Caesar was thirty years old, he hadn't accomplished much of anything. He was a local delegate, but hardly the iconic figure he would go on to become. What changed? He visited Alexandria and saw the giant statue of Alexander. He had never seen anything like that. He dropped to his knees and wept. When he stood up and wiped his tears, he returned to Rome and spent the next thirty years of his life charging ahead on his path to become one of the most famous rulers in history. Caesar experienced the Law of Environmental Exposure that day at Alexandria, and it changed him forever in the most profound of ways.

I was twenty years old when I stopped playing college basketball. At that point in my life, I was a different person than who I am now. I was confused about what I wanted to with my life. I thought opening my own gym might be fun or maybe going to chiropractic school. Without realizing it, I was still sifting and sorting through the dreams and expectations of others, instead of my own.

One weekend, I attended a marketing event in New Jersey, just hoping to find a spark or something to push me in a certain direction. I ended up meeting a twenty-six-year-old guy named Joel Marion. At the time, I was drawn to him, but I didn't fully understand why. Now I know: he was high status. He had a purpose, he was decisive, he was certainty in motion, and he was in power. As I talked to him, I was blown away by his story. In the span of one year, he had gone from a high school gym teacher in New Jersey to running an online business that made him $350,000 in a month. It blew my mind.

Joel Marion is a great guy, and we're still good friends

today. He's one of the most succinct and straightforward speakers I've ever known. When I asked him how he made the successful transition from nondescript gym teacher to accomplished online businessman, he told me his steps before leaving me with two pieces of advice: don't get complicated and don't listen to other people.

As a broke twenty-year-old with no high-status destiny, I was fucking pumped. I left that event completely invigorated. Within the first month after applying what he told me, I had an online business as a basketball trainer that made me $20,000 a month. The business did well. As a former college basketball player myself, I was able to help more than 1,000 players. It was a win-win for everyone, but I made a major mistake. I got totally comfortable making that kind of money and I coasted. By the time I was twenty-three, I was broke again and had to move back to my parents' house and rebuild my life. After retooling myself once again, I moved back out to California and eventually met another guy in his midtwenties with an online business pulling in $150,000 a month. I had the same feeling of amazement as when I had met Joel Marion a few years prior. After learning some of his tips and techniques, my own profits skyrocketed from about $15,000 a month to $100,000 a month within 150 days.

I share all of this with you not to brag, but to introduce

the concept of environmental exposure. Everyone who achieves success has specific visceral moments in life where they meet someone in person, not online or through a book. To be able to shake that person's hand, feel their energy, and speak directly with them can change your entire concept of what's possible. I could have read the same information Joel Marion shared with me in a book, but it wouldn't have had the same effect. This is why I encourage my most motivated people not just to read this book, but also to take my video course and attend a live event. You deserve the best, and you deserve these life-changing experiences. We call these experiences "environmental exposures," and they're critically important to your success.

LAW OF SUSTAINED EXPOSURE

The major moments that create environmental exposures can transform your entire point of view, but you need long-term factors to make sure you stay at that same level. You can't count on seeing Joel Marion every day, right? This is the Law of Sustained Exposure, and for it to work, you must remove any factors that bring you down.

Bedros Keuilian, one of my good friends and business partners, was in Alaska on a family trip a few years ago. One day, he was walking around on a fishing dock when

FAST ACTION EXERCISE: HIGH-STATUS SELF-LOVE

We all know the importance of self-love. You can't give love to others if you don't have it for yourself. All high-status people love themselves. It's at the crux of their effervescent being.

One of my favorite questions to ask clients, students, and customers alike is, "What are some things that you do for the people you love?" After they write down their list, I ask them a simple follow-up question: "Are you doing those things for yourself?" One of the fastest ways to increase self-love is to start doing for yourself the things you do for those you love.

I'm a huge proponent of thought loops. I do them all the time, and I recommend you do, too. Sometimes I'll just look in the mirror and go on a rant for a minute or two about why I love myself. It's not to impress anyone or call attention to myself. It's for me alone. It's fun to tell yourself all of the reasons why you love yourself and why you deserve love.

One of my favorite exercises at live events is something called the "self-love letter." We have everyone in attendance write a love letter to themselves, then fold it up, kiss it, and put it in an envelope. On that envelope, they write their address, seal it, and give it to us. Ninety days later we mail it back to them. By that point, they've forgotten about it completely, so it catches them by surprise. It's an emotional, powerful experience to read a love letter from yourself, and it's something I want you to have too.

STEP 1
Write a love letter to yourself, fold it up, kiss it and put it in an envelope.

STEP 2
Store the envelope somewhere safe where you won't be tempted to open it, and set a note on your calendar to reopen the envelope just thirty days from now.

STEP 3
Open it back up after thirty days and read it to yourself. You'll be amazed what you feel. Some people who do this end up in tears of joy and gratitude while reading, so be ready for a wave of emotion to overcome and lift your spirits even more.

he struck up a conversation with a local fisherman. The guy had different buckets everywhere, but it was a bucket of crabs that caught Bedros's attention. He noticed one superambitious crab climbing, mustering every ounce of strength in its little body to pull itself higher and higher. Bedros was entranced. Finally, he turned to the fisherman and said, "Dude, you might want to look at this. One of your crabs is about to escape." The fisherman just smiled. "No, don't worry. Watch what happens next." Right on cue, Bedros watched as the other crabs in the bucket reached up and grabbed the ambitious one's little legs and yanked him back down to the bottom. Bedros just lost it. "Wow, that is life! That is what people do to each other. That's the perfect metaphor."

That poor little crab lived in an environment that was, quite literally, bringing him down. You don't mean to be that crab, forever trying to escape from a bucket that keeps pulling you back down. What are the types of things that pull us down? Obviously, we're not exactly like crabs. Other humans typically aren't pulling us to the floor. But there are a few red flags to watch out for. Environments with lots of gossip and constant interruptions will bring you down. Eleanor Roosevelt once said, "Great minds discuss ideas; average minds discuss events; small minds discuss people." You want an environment that promotes talk about positive, new ideas, not gossip about other people or events. Likewise, you need an environment that doesn't interrupt you while you're working. There was a study done that found the average worker is interrupted every three minutes and fifty seconds. About half of these interruptions are self-inflicted—social media, cell phones, etc.—and the other half are inflicted by others. These are the things that bring you down.

POWER OF ENVIRONMENT

We've all heard the expression, "You're the average of the five people that you hang around." It's an old personal-development philosophy and, honestly, it's misleading to a lot of people new to the game. There's nothing special about the number five. It's important to delete old methods of thinking like this from your brain. The truth is that you're the average of the people you associate most with. It's not limited to just five, and it's certainly not limited to just people you physically see. If you're reading a 1,000-page Steve Jobs biography and it's been weighing on your mind for weeks, you are mentally associating with him.

My mentor Dan Peña taught me a simple saying about this. He said, "Show me your friends and I'll show you your future." Most successful people tend to get this instinctively, and that was the case with Frank Sinatra. The Rat Pack was created because Sinatra consciously decided he wanted to have people around him all the time that had something he wanted himself. He wanted a guy like Dean Martin because he was the epitome of cool. He wanted a guy like Sammy Davis Jr. so he could increase his showmanship. He wanted some power, so he befriended people in the Mafia. If you were a unique person, Sinatra wanted you around so he could study you up close.

Oprah Winfrey is also known to keep a close council of valuable people around her. How about the President of the United States? Every President has an entire cabinet of counselors and advisors. The real question is this: Are the lives of Sinatra, Oprah, and the President more important than yours? Of course not. So, if they're going to keep valuable people around them, why wouldn't you? Like Warren Buffet says, "It's better to hang out with people better than you." Everyone is judged on the company they keep in life, so pick out associates whose behavior is even better than yours, and you will follow in their direction.

The right high-status environment will also help keep your hunger value high. What's hunger value? Simple. Let's say you set a goal of making $1 million in a year. If you reach that goal, what happens next? Do you lose that hunger and simply become content with maintaining at the same level? Or do you stay hungry and push yourself even harder? You want your environment to keep that hunger value high, and that happens by surrounding yourself with people who are also hungry.

Simply by spending time around people and watching them operate in their area of expertise is the fastest way to learn. Osmosis, which is absorbing knowledge by watching and then mimicking someone, is incredibly effective. If someone gave you a book on how to shoot free throws in basketball, you would never learn as quickly or as effectively as if you simply watched Stephen Curry shoot for twenty minutes in person. I ask the same question to all my clients who think simply reading more books is the answer. How many books do you need to read before you can become an accurate marksman? Osmosis works best because it takes advantage of the same method medical schools use in clinical training: see one, do one, teach one.

In online business, there are two keys to making things work—traffic and conversion. You've got to get people to your website and then convert them into customers. I held an event in early 2015 and two of the guys in attendance were perfect for each other. One of them was excellent at driving traffic, while the other was a conversion expert. They both struggled in the other area of online business. They met at my event, ended up forming a business partnership after being exposed to each other through osmosis, and ended up learning together. Within sixty days, their joint business venture had exploded. They came back to another event a few months later and showed me pictures of their matching Ferrari. Osmosis is a powerful tool. Surround yourself with people you can watch and learn from.

BUILDING HIGH-STATUS ENVIRONMENT

We know what a high-status environment consists of, but how do we create it? What are the factors that go into setting it up? Let's start with a two-step high-status environmental workshop.

STEP 1: REMOVE CRABS PHYSICALLY

List every single person you have associated with over the last week. Every person you've talked with, texted with, e-mailed with, thought about—write them all down. It helps to just check your phone and go through your texts, calls, Instagram messages, and Snapchats from the last week. Put them all on the list.

When you have your list in front of you, identify which people don't directly support your goals. Put check marks next to their names. Everyone left on the list should be people who directly support your goals. Circle all of their names.

If you want to ensure you achieve more of your goals than you've imagined and in less time than you thought you could, the people with check marks have to go. It may sound cold, but the reality is they're already freezing you in motion, and it's not helping you. They are the crabs pulling you back down to the bottom of the barrel. And remember, removing them from your environment might not mean you'll never see them again. It just might mean you have to limit your exposure to them, or at least consciously select times, places, and events to enjoy with them where you know they'll be in a positive mood instead of crablike.

If this feels a bit scary for you, just remember that it's not permanent. There's nothing to say they can't come back into your life down the road, but for now, as you make these giant shifts in your life to become high status and pursue your dreams, you just can't have people blocking your path.

STEP 2: REMOVE CRABS MENTALLY

Opinions are like nostrils—everyone has at least two. How can you possibly move forward in your own life if you're being weighed down or yanked around by all these opinions? It's impossible. No successful man or woman in the history of the world allowed themselves to be surrounded by negativity, distractions, or predictions that disempower them. We're going to rewire your mental environment for bigger, better, faster success by first answering a question.

Who are the four people you admire most? There is no right answer here. This is totally personal to you. I just want you to write them down now. Take a few minutes if you have to, and it is OK if you don't know them personally. One of my greatest heroes and people I admire most is Benjamin Franklin. Sad to say, but I never got to meet Big Ben.

When you have your list of four people, take a good look at it. Now you have a new rule: the opinions of the people on this list matter most to you. Their opinions now weigh a ton. Anybody not fortunate enough to have made your exclusive list? Their opinions are nothing more than flatulence in a tornado. I like to carry my own list around with me, and remind myself every once in a while what matters most and what does not. If someone uninformed and not on the list attempts to share their opinion with me, I will stop them sometimes and say, "Hey, I appreciate it, but unfortunately, you're not on the list. Have a great day though." Plus, when you want to seek mentorship, guidance, or advice, you now have a concrete list of masters to turn to.

LIVE EVENTS

Most people go to the same six places over and over—their house, work, coffee place, gym, favorite restaurant, and bar. I highly recommend you add one more crucial place to that list if you're going to rise up and live your dreams. That seventh addition is live events. Have you ever stopped to wonder, "Where are all the people who think like me?" They are at live events. What types of live events? Seminars, workshops, conferences, expos—they're all great because you will meet and connect with so many new, like-minded people. This is one of the many reasons so many men and women sign up to attend one of our own events. They want to try it out, and they end up coming back many, many times. They wouldn't do that unless they were getting something truly valuable out of it.

COACHING

Receiving coaching is taking advantage of the Law of Sustained Exposure in the ultimate fashion. Even Alexander himself had a coach, and it was none other than Aristotle, the legendary Greek philosopher. Now, unfortunately, we can't visit Aristotle's website and see what kind of coaching he's offering, but this serves as an important reminder—coaching from a person will always offer you something bigger than books can.

The best never stop learning, either. Leonardo DiCaprio, who is widely recognized as one of the best actors in the world, still has an acting coach. When Warren Buffet decided he wanted to become a great bridge player, he didn't read dozens of books or study online videos. He got a fucking coach.

READ MORE, WATCH LESS

I've been saying that absorbing knowledge and information through osmosis is far more effective than reading books, and that's still true. But that doesn't mean you *shouldn't* read books. People read, on average, ten books for the rest of their lives after they finish college. That is one of the scariest statistics I've ever learned.

I'm a bibliophile. I love books, and I know how impactful they can be. One book can change your life. People turn away from books later in life because they were trained as kids to associate them with pain. Reading was homework and thus a form of punishment. It's a shame.

I'm going to share a quick excerpt from *No B.S. Time Management for Entrepreneurs*, a book written by legendary direct-response marketing guru and rabid reader Dan Kennedy:

You must read a lot to succeed. Here are the reasons. Number one, varied, diverse input, ideas, viewpoints, life stories, examples, all the essential raw material poured into your subconscious mind for it to sift, sort, try matching up with other puzzle pieces it already has, so it can occasionally yell, "Eureka!" and hand you something profitable or exciting without daily flow of new stuff it just sleeps. Wealth secret, a bonus wealth secret, you cannot manufacture anything without raw material, not even money. Two, without exposure to others' thinking your own range of thought shrinks. Soon you are a mental midget. Your range of thought narrows like range of motion shrinks if you don't move and don't stretch. Three, you can't stay current.

I read a monstrous amount and I still can't stay current. If you're not reading a book or two or a dozen magazines, a few newspapers, and a few newsletters every week, you must be way, way, way behind. Pretty soon your conversation reveals you to be a dinosaur. Fourth, if you have kids you want to set decent example for them. They need to see you reading. They need to hear you talking about what you read. When I was a kid, the years my family was dead broke, we made a regular scheduled weekly trek to the public library for an hour or so. My father, mother and I each picked out three or four books for the week. We took them home and we read them and we talked about them. Now today I prefer going to the book store because I have the money and I like keeping the books. However, I'm grateful for the library habit years. It would be a better thing for most families to do than going to the movies, the arcade or Walmart.

If you don't already, start reading books with regularity. Another option to consider is audio and video courses. Video courses come with visual aids, which gives you a better chance to model the person you're seeing. But audio courses are perfect when you're driving in the car. Listening to an audio course is going to be far more beneficial for you than listening to the nonsense on the radio.

In that same sense, TV is terrible for you. At its core, it programs you to be fearful and low status. Worst of all, the mainstream media mostly focuses on the product, not the process. When you watch a celebrity show on the glitz and glamour of their life, you're not seeing the effort, tears, sweat, and work that went into building all of that. It embeds the ideas that celebrities are special people who have something you don't, and probably can never have. Which, of course, is bullshit. You have everything you need inside of you right now to pursue your dreams and make them a reality. Trust me, celebrities don't have any unique fairy dust sprinkled on them that makes them special. Most are not special. Some are though, and they are the ones who have worked their ass off to build a legacy. Normal TV sucks. Period. Be kind to yourself and try to avoid it altogether, if possible.

THE INSTRUCTIVE DEAD

Read biographies of successful men and women throughout history. Doing this will allow you to learn their personal secrets to success. See it, hear it, touch it, feel it. Allow their hard-earned, wise, proven points of view to become your POV. It will start to seep into your own and create a synergistic effect for you.

Again, this is the osmosis effect in action. Figure out who's really interesting to you and start reading about their life. You will be shocked and delighted at how many of the challenges they faced on a daily basis are similar to your own.

PRIMING

Priming is a fascinating subject in behavioral science. Here's the short of it: If I have you hold a warm cup of coffee, you are going to be a warmer, kinder version of yourself for a short period of time. If I have you hold an iced coffee, you are going to be a colder, more distant version of yourself for a period of time. This concept can be seen in many areas that our conscious brain would never recognize. For instance, images of unity temporarily make you more cooperative, symbols of wealth temporarily make you more ambitious, and pictures of delicious food temporarily make you feel hungry.

What we want to do is place items in your environment that will prime you for the attitudes and traits you want magnified in yourself. Alexander the Great, for example, slept every night with two items that had a priming effect for him—a copy of *The Odyssey* and a dagger, which he kept under his pillow. That's how he primed his environment, but you don't have to go that far.

Start with the following exercise: What are three things in your work environment right now that just don't help you? They might be things that trigger negative memories, distract you, or even symbolize laziness and sloth. We've got to get rid of those negative primers. You are not a tree, stuck in one place. You can move, and if there are things that aren't helping you, you can donate them or just throw them out. Rid your environment of those three items now. They are only hurting your success, even if you are not consciously aware of it.

Now, let's keep it going with the next step: What are three things you know could inspire you to take more action or remind you to continue training and ingraining your high-status signals? It could be pictures of people, a meaningful object, something from a great past memory. We want to replace those three negative items you just removed with these three positive primers. You don't have to stop at just three, but start small at first. You're going to find the simple act of swapping three items will make an instant difference in your output, mind-set, and energy. Weeks from now, your environment is going to look completely different, and finally, it will be working in your favor, instead of against you.

VALUE YOURSELF ABOVE OTHERS

Don't spend time with anyone who devalues your intention to evolve. It is your duty to succeed, and anyone who is not supporting that simply cannot stay if they continue that course of behavior. I'll share one last personal story here as it relates to high-status environment. A few years ago, one of my closest friends turned thirty years old, but he was still drifting through life. We hadn't been able to see each other as much as in the past, with him living in Florida and me in California. We kept in touch though, and I saw him drifting at thirty, still doing the same things he was when he was twenty-five years old.

It came to a point where I had to change something. I wasn't being a good friend by allowing him to stay on that path. I told him, "Listen, dude, we're not going to talk for a while. I hope that you can make this shift in your own maturity and your own transformation, and you can keep growing because that's what I want most for you. I feel like me being friends with you at this point is not doing it." He didn't understand at first, and I knew he wouldn't. He tried calling, texting, and e-mailing me. He had mutual friends reach out to me on his behalf. Even though I wanted to get back in touch with him, I stuck to my guns.

About six months after that, I bumped into him a marketing event. The change was instantly apparent. He had lost twenty pounds, he was dressed well, and he was sharp in conversation. He told me he had stopped drinking and had made six figures in six months after previously only bringing in a few thousand dollars per month.

I would never take credit for his transformation, because he's the one who did the work, but he did tell me my decision pushed him to truly evaluate his life and think, "One of my best friends isn't talking to me right now. Not because I did something, but because I haven't been chasing my potential to its edge. This is my wake-up call."

CONCLUSION

We have come a *long* way together. How much further you're going to go from here will be your decision. This book has given you the tools—the signals of higher status with ideas, techniques, exercises, and technology—that can absolutely change your life in an instant, just like they have for so many others on the planet. When you put this book down, you're likely going to feel a surging sense of excitement, but maybe also a sense of concern.

You now know information no one else does, which presents an opportunity. This opportunity comes in the form of a few questions: Where will you go from here? How much higher status do you want to become? What great things will you achieve as you become increasingly higher status? How many more people will you inspire and impact because of your high status? Challenge yourself to answer these questions as you move forward.

Or, you can put the book down and forget everything you have learned here. You can go back to being the way you were, floating through life like a leaf in the wind. If there's one thing I can be certain about more than anything else, it's that we only get one life. Like Steve Jobs said, "Life isn't a second chance. It's your only chance." To me, the absolute greatest failure someone can have is to possess the keys to change their life for the better and create the life they want for themselves, yet do nothing with them. I know you're not that kind of person, and I know you're not going do that.

WHAT'S NEXT?

You've learned how to peel back the layers of the onion to discover your deeper purpose, your destiny in life. You've learned simple, yet powerful and effective tricks to change the way you walk, sit, talk, and connect with people. You've learned how to live a carefree life, how to give truth in a way that strengthens relationships, and how to captivate attention with your style and charisma. So, let me ask you: What high-status direction are you heading in right now?

Where is your life going? Is it headed in the way you want? Is it headed somewhere in the middle? Are you partially still living a life that other people wanted for you and partially living a life that you want for yourself? Or are you a full-frontal gangster? Have you committed to a destiny for yourself that turns you on, that lights you up, that looks, sounds, and smells incredible to you? Have you committed to a destiny that the mere thought of makes you feel passionate, excited, and inspired? Is your life heading in that direction, or not? This is the perfect time for you to take a step back if it's not, and really ask yourself what needs to change.

If I were to shoot two arrows from the same bow and one was headed just one degree higher than the other, over a few feet you wouldn't be able to tell a difference in their trajectory. If you watched a few hundred feet more, you would start to notice a small difference. If you tracked them miles ahead, the difference would be enormous. If you tracked them even longer than that, at some point you would realize you couldn't even tell that both arrows came from the same bow. The direction of your life works the exact same way. One small degree of change can affect everything.

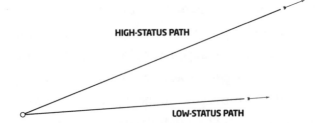

A mentor once told me, "In relationships, business with friends, or romantic things, these relationships, they don't fail overnight, OK? They fail over a series of small, correctable failures." You need to ensure that the path of your arrow is on target because one-degree failures can mean a world of different results that you aren't aiming for. You need to ensure your arrow is not only on target, but that you're making the right decisions every day to keep the arrow in the right direction.

Look out for distractions. Even as you build your high-status environment, you're not going to have complete control over it. Things will pop up, and they're going to serve as tests for you. Tests to see if you can be seduced off your high-status path into a direction that maybe isn't quite so good for you. When those tests arise, you need to pass them. John Wooden, arguably the greatest coach in the modern world, taught all his players, "If you do it once, you'll do it twice." He taught them to play defense a certain way, in which they always had one hand in front of the player they were guarding and the other hand guarding the passing lane. If even for one play a player decided, "You know what? I'm fatigued. I'm tired. This game's already over. I don't need to put my hands up here. I can relax," if they allowed themselves to do it once, they would certainly do it twice. Pretty soon, it's not just something you do sometimes. It's the new habit. It's the new way of doing things.

We have a saying here on Team Capital. You don't make exceptions to a rule, you just make a new rule. When you make an exception to a rule, you think you're doing it just once, but you're not. You're actually creating an entirely new rule. You're changing the game. You've changed the rules, and if you do it once, you'll do it twice. You need to make sure that every step of the way when these tests arise, you don't just say, "You know what? I'll just do it this one time," because you won't be doing it just one time. You'll be changing the direction of your arrow, and you'll end up in a place where you don't want to be.

WHO WILL YOU BE?

You know by now there are three types of people—high status, neutral status, and low status. Low-status people wouldn't be here reading this right now. They would've read the first page of this book and realized, "Holy shit, this is way too powerful. This could change my life, but change is scary. I'm just going to put this book down, walk away, pretend like I never saw it, put my head down and go back to living my life with my eyes closed."

A high-status person would be raring to get started on their mission in life after reading this book, raring to take action and make progress on their path. For them, the action starts now. A neutral-status person would probably still be reading at this point, but they'd be unsure. Unsure about their path, unsure about themselves, unsure if they're doing it right. If that's you, this is your time to choose. This is your time to decide. This is your time to make a ripple in still water and decide what kind of effect you're going to create.

High status is a choice, and it's one you need to make now. You need to make a commitment—not to me, but to yourself—that you are going to continue to increase your status every single day with tiny, bite-size increments of progress and improvement. We call that *kaizen*, which is Japanese for "improvement." If you trust the process, you'll see how the constant small improvements lead to massive growth over time.

Are you ready to commit? I hope so, because I'm not going

to let you go to the next sentence until you decide right now. I want you to say out loud, "I am a high-status individual." Say it! Now. Don't wait. I don't care if someone's around you. I don't care if it's weird. Be weird. Say it out loud. "I am high status." Did you? Good.

Now that you've made this commitment to yourself, I want to invite you to take the next step: get on a team. In fact, get on multiple teams. We know how important the Law of Environmental Exposure and the Law of Sustained Exposure are. Remember, we need both. We need those big environmental exposures to really reset our standards and change our set points for what's possible, and we need those sustained exposures to keep us grounded. Be conscious of your old environment and don't fall prey to those who used to pull you down. You've got to get on teams with high-status people and surround yourself with positive people who will continue to raise you up.

THE POWER IS REAL

I also want you to share the information you've learned with others. Not the whole book—there's no way you could remember everything, and I don't expect you to. But share the stuff that's been most powerful for you. I want you to share it with others for two reasons. First, research shows that when you share information with others, it helps you learn it faster and on a deeper level. The more you teach it to others, the better you're going to be able to remember, practice, and use this knowledge. Second, there's just a certain joy that comes from helping others. There will be a certain richness added to the quality of your life when you are consistently helping other people. It isn't giving advice just to get one-up in a conversation. You're sharing proven, actionable knowledge that they've never heard of, that they've never seen before, that is going to create an instant positive change in their life. When you see that change and you see that smile erupt on their face, you're going to feel a sense of joy rush through you. I want that for you.

I was teaching a sold-out workshop recently and after two straight twelve-hour days, I was exhausted. I remember sitting backstage, drinking tea, and talking with my team when one of the students came up to me. Normally, we're busy working during those breaks, but I could tell there was something different about this guy. He was holding a big blue gift with both hands. I had no idea what it was and when I asked him, he showed it to me and said, "Jason, it took me a lot of courage and a lot of time to actually show this to you and share this with you and tell you the story, but I have to now. I have the courage and the confidence to share it with you now comfortably. I've been in the Marines for the last few years, and while I was there, very early on I was kind of bullied by a lot of people and it really got me down. It really made me feel bad. It really made me think some thoughts that weren't good for me, but I found you. I don't even know how I found you and the concept of status, but it changed my life. It changed me completely.

"The way I moved, the way I talked, the way I looked, the way I acted, the way I thought about everything. My energy, my confidence, my positivity. Everything transformed as a result of status and as a result of that, not only did these bullies stop doing that to me, but they actually became not only good friends of mine, but guys who looked to me for advice and for leadership. They followed me. At one point early on, I was very seriously considering just ending my life, and status stopped me from doing that. It changed everything for me, and I just wanted to thank you with this gift because you saved my life."

He opened the gift and it was a giant blue quilt that he created, and stitched into the fabric at the top it said, "Jason Capital saved a Marine's life." It was amazing. All the exhaustion I felt disappeared as I was just overcome with happiness and joy. I don't get teary-eyed very often, but that was an incredible moment. I told him, "Listen, I didn't do anything. You did it, but thank you for saying that." He's now out of the Marines and is writing his first book. He's living his high-status destiny.

My mom visited the Capital Compound not long after that happened and she saw the quilt, which we have proudly displayed on the wall. As I told her the story, tears started to stream down her face and I told her, "Mom, anyone could've done what I did. You don't have to cry. If it hadn't been me, it would've been someone else." "But Jason," she said, "it wasn't someone else. It was you."

IT'S YOUR TIME

Be a doer, not a talker. Be an action-taker, a leader. In life, I've discovered there are two kinds of people—ducks and eagles. Eagles soar through the sky and hunt their prey. They fiercely protect their families and move with purpose and pride. Ducks, on the other hand, just waddle around quacking. They talk a lot, but they move slowly and don't get a lot done. Don't be a fucking duck. You've got to be an eagle. I want you to soar.

My final challenge to you as we wrap up here is to keep *kaizen*-ing. Continue to become higher and higher status every day. Keep self-correcting, and never judge yourself at any point along the way. Enjoy finding ways that you can get better, finding ways that you can grow, finding new ways to love, finding ways to achieve things you never thought you could. Set goals so grand that you can't achieve them in this lifetime, so you remain passionate, excited, and constantly evolving throughout the course of your life.

Did you know that most people who open a book never finish it? Can you imagine that? What if most people who ran a marathon never finished all 26.2 miles? That's what more than 90 percent of people do when they start a book. They don't finish it. You are *not* one of them. You are a high-status individual. You've made it here to the end and for that, I thank you.

I also want to thank you for your commitment to yourself, for your commitment to me, and for your commitment to becoming the highest-status version of yourself. I want you to keep going, because I hope to see you at one of my future events and hear how your life has changed for the better, or you accomplished an amazing personal goal, or you helped a family member. Whatever it is, I want to hear it, so I can go back onstage and share it with thousands of other people. I would love to one day tell *your* success story.

John Wooden was once given advice by a mentor when he was very young, and to me it's some of the best advice I've ever heard. It's almost a blessing. Wooden was told, "Be true to yourself, help others, make each day your master-piece, make friendship a fine art, drink deeply from good books, build a shelter against a rainy day, give thanks for your blessings and pray for guidance every day."

May you enjoy the ascent and excitement of the beautiful path that awaits you, my friend. Until we meet again, bon voyage.

ACKNOWLEDGMENTS

This isn't easy. As I began to think of all the people I wanted to express my appreciation for, in their support and guidance of my growth and evolution, the list continued to grow.

First, I would like to thank my girlfriend Nataly for supporting and nourishing my creative output, which strikes at all hours of the day and night, whether we're at home in Newport Coast or cruising inside a speedboat through the blue-water canals of Venice.

Next, I'd like to thank my dear friend and business partner Bedros Keuilian. He truly is the "hidden genius" behind many of the world's most successful brands and faces, and his continued guidance, support, and mentorship has been incredibly impactful for me. We are building something truly amazing together, my friend.

To Dan Peña, the 50 Billion Dollar Man, for your incredible energy and passion for sharing your wisdom.

Taylor Layne, for your excellent work and obsession with *kaizen* and always making everything better. Imagine what we're going to be creating and how many we're going to touch worldwide now. Amazing.

To Z, Steve Ovens, Brent Turner, Jad, Samuel, Steven, Tiffany, and the rest of our team, I would not be able to do what I do if not for all that you do.

To Craig Ballantyne, for being the first one to tell me I had something special as an entrepreneur.

To my friends David Sinick, John Romaniello, and Adam Gilad. You guys are incredible, and our times together are treasured.

Of course, the book could never have existed without the efforts of Kathleen Pedersen, Brad Kauffman, Kevin Murphy, Andrew Lovell, and the rest of the team at Lion-crest Publishing. You guys were incredible and on point every step of the way.

To my first mentor, Jonny Kest. Your wisdom continues to blossom for me today, and it has been a privilege to share some of what I learned from you, years ago, as a teenager, with millions of people around the globe.

To the men and women who inspired and continue to inspire my work from afar. To me, this is my favorite then, when someone's actions, their shining commitment to their own path illuminates your own. Steve Nash. Benjamin Franklin. The great Charlie Munger. Robert Downey Jr.

To the most inspirational women I've ever had the pleasure of learning about, Helen Keller. I want a slice of your courage when I grow up.

And finally, to the hundreds of thousands of Team Capital members worldwide. Your action, your self-love, your value-giving mentality are going to help us make this world much, much better for those who come after.

ABOUT THE AUTHOR

JASON CAPITAL is founder and chairman of Capital Research International. For eleven years, he has served as coach and consultant to Fortune 500 executives, professional athletes, Navy SEALs, best-selling authors, and Hollywood luminaries. He has been recognized as a Top 100 Entrepreneur by President Barack Obama.